Best
White

Best White

And Other Anxious Delusions

Rebecca Davis

MACMILLAN

First published in 2015
by Pan Macmillan South Africa
Private Bag x19
Northlands
Johannesburg
2116

www.panmacmillan.co.za

ISBN 978-1-77010-415-0
e-ISBN 978-1-77010-416-7

Editing by Tanya Pampalone
Proofreading by Sally Hines
Design and typesetting by Triple M Design
Cover design by K4
Cover photograph of the rosette by iStockphoto

Printed and bound by Creda Communications

To my family
And to Jeanine, without whom there would be no book

Contents

1

Always Wash Your Fruit

People rarely ask me for life advice. I suspect this may be because I occasionally wear the same clothes for several days at a time.

I do, however, have one extremely important nugget of acquired learning. I sometimes feel that I should whisper it to strangers on the street, and then walk away with the glad step of someone secure in the knowledge that they have changed a life for the better.

Without beating around the bush any further: you should always wash your fruit and vegetables.

There is often an almost tangible sense of anticlimax amongst listeners when I unburden myself of this advice. I am aware that literally everyone gets told to wash their fruit and vegetables. There's even a sticker on your lettuce packet that reminds you. But believe me when I say that this is not one of those 'optional' life instructions, like flossing your teeth or washing your jeans. You really, really have to.

I know this as plainly as I know my own name because I once worked in a fruit-packing factory. It was in the early years of the 2000s, when the rand was so weak that South Africans could pop over to the UK, spend a few weeks cleaning toilets at McDonald's, and return to buy a wine farm in cash. It was something like when the Brits found out about diamonds in Kimberley in the 1800s, only the other way round.

Being hungry for our own wine farm – and just for wine, really – my twin sister Rachel and I resolved to cash in on this latter-day gold rush. It was the end of our third year at university, when the world still lies before you all dappled and promise-rich. A pretty casual online search threw up a website called fruityjobs.com, which assured us that our fortune was to be made in picking and packing English fruit.

In retrospect, this sounds like the kind of promise that only peasants in the Great Depression would fall for. Not true. As educated, middle-class metropolitans, we found the invitation deeply alluring. We packed two nice wheelie-bag suitcases full of two-minute noodles and tuna – for the first bit, we reasoned, just to carry us over until our fruity fortunes kicked in – and flew off to England in high spirits. Mid-winter.

What we arrived at was not a sun-drenched orchard, but a bleak, waterlogged farm cowering under the shadow of towering electricity pylons. Work took place in a freezing warehouse lined with long trestle tables beneath flickery neon light strips. In front of us, muddy strawberry plants were piled next to guillotines. We were required to grab each plant, slice off extraneous foliage and tie them in bundles of 12.

This sounds like a task a demented chimp could perform with its eyes closed, but in reality it was not. Our hands were bloated and frozen with cold much of the time, like big pink hams freshly extracted from a freezer. It made any precise digital manoeuvring – like tying knots – difficult to manage. Then there was the fact that, as a pair of 20-year-old blonde twins, we were the object of some fascination in the warehouse. It wasn't our looks that drew attention. Speaking frankly, we weren't looking our very best, since we had to wear all the clothes we'd brought in our wheelie bags every day to stave off hypothermia. It was also much too cold to consider showering.

No, it was simply that we stood out quite a lot, because every single other worker was a male refugee from Iraq.

'You have husband?' they would take turns to sidle up and ask. Beggars can't be choosers: since we possessed the only vaginas within a 20-mile radius, they had to overlook how closely we resembled smelly Michelin Men.

'Yes! Definitely!' we would snap defensively. We were lying. They knew we were lying. It was obvious. What self-respecting Western man would send his woman out looking like a homeless astronaut every day to pluck at soiled vegetation with asylum-seekers?

Their flirting techniques might have lacked finesse, but they could chop the shit out of strawberry plants. Their hands were a blur of fluid movement, while we hacked away like remedial lumberjacks. Every now and then they would mutter to each other while staring fixedly at us and then laugh uproariously. We agreed it was probably something along the lines of: 'Which one will crack first for a hand-job?'

We would have been far more generously disposed to consider dispensing manual stimulation if they had offered to help us meet the farm's Stalinist daily targets. When we arrived at work each morning, the target for the day would be starkly chalked on a board. Day after day, the numbers escalated like a spiralling nightmare. 'TODAY'S TARGET: 70 BUNCHES', we would read as we entered, mouthing the words in horror. They might as well have written 'TODAY'S TARGET: BUILD A FUNCTIONING SPACE SHUTTLE OUT OF BITS OF CHOPPED-UP STRAWBERRY'.

Our co-workers surpassed the targets effortlessly. To us they seemed absurdly unreachable, however much we coaxed our gammon hands to chop and tie faster. If the setting had been a North Korean labour camp, after a few days we would definitely have been hauled to the front of the warehouse and executed as an example.

The main problem, however, was not the shame of not meeting the targets. It was that we were paid per bundle, at a rate that dropped without warning each day. It was like being a worker in Zimbabwe during hyper-inflation. We had to get out.

We called fruityjobs.com from a payphone. They wanted nothing to do with us. It was a brutal approach, but perhaps a fair one. We hadn't exactly covered ourselves with glory in our first foray into the fruit industry. The internet presented another possibility. It was time to advance within the sector. We were choppers and bundlers no longer; our future lay in packing.

The new job took place at a factory on the industrialised outskirts of a city in Kent. It was warmer inside, which was a big plus. Sexual harassment rates were also marginally down because in our uniform of oversized blue overalls and hairnets we were barely recognisable as human, never mind female.

We packed small fruit – berries, mainly – for supermarkets. If you were careful to remain undetected, you could sneak fistfuls of berries into your mouth at regular intervals while you packed the fruit into their punnets. In this way we learnt the magical properties of each berry, like feral children scouring a forest for sustenance. Take blueberries, for example: a natural sedative.

One day two young Brits joined the assembly line. Giving weight to every stereotype about English nutrition, they were not well-versed in the world of fruit. Indeed, they treated each new specimen as some curious, alien life form.

'What d'you call this then, Kev?' one would ask, rolling a piece of fruit between her fingers and holding it up to the light to inspect.

'I reckon those are ... cherries?' Kev would hazard doubtfully.

The most onerous job was weighing the fruit to ensure that the right quantity ended up in each container. You'd fill a punnet and anxiously wait for the scale needle to settle. It would be over the prescribed weight by a few milligrams, so you'd remove one single berry. Too light. You'd add a different berry. Too heavy. Another promisingly sized berry would have to be selected. After a few hours you'd start losing your grip on reality altogether, especially if you'd been steadily stuffing your face with blueberries.

Sometimes I would fantasise about hiding little notes in the packaging. 'Please help, I am an alienated worker trapped in a fruit-packing factory,' they might read. 'An all-fruit diet loosens the bowels something awful.' By this time we had eaten all the noodles and tuna from our wheelie bags, and beyond berry-plundering we were surviving largely on occasional forkfuls of biryani extended as a gesture of charity from the elderly Punjabi women we worked with. It was absurdly kind of them to donate food to us, considering that the factory work constituted their permanent employment, rather than being a whimsical holiday job for spoiled white South Africans.

More than a decade later, I was tickled to read a news story about a disgruntled English baker who covertly slipped haikus into packets of Sainsbury's biscuits for consumers to find. A typical offering: 'Enjoy your cookies/Every bite is a minute/I'll never get back'. I'm not saying the author didn't have legitimate grievances, but biscuit manufacturing seems a notable step up from fruit packing. Imagine the mounds of choc chips that they would have access to.

Our quality of life outside the factory walls was also compromised by the fact that we were living in a trailer park. Sometimes the liquid in my contact lens holders would partially freeze overnight. We shared our chilly caravan with a man called Sunil, who had a criminal record for grievous bodily harm. On trips to the supermarket you had to give him a wide berth at the checkout because he had an embarrassing habit of shop-lifting marmalade. But he was a soft soul at heart, proud of the fact that he'd taught his cat how to open doors. In retrospect, this might have been so the cat could join him in a life of crime.

Objectively assessed, it was all a bit shit, really. But after a few weeks, something unexpected happened: I started quite seriously enjoying the work. I'd arrive at the factory each morning hoping to be assigned to stickering, which was my favourite task. The little boxes of berries would trundle down the assembly line, and when they reached you, you'd slap a label on each one. Again, this doesn't sound like a particularly challenging form of labour, but it had to be undertaken at incredible speed. If you missed a box because you were fumbling with your sticker roll, it could cause a pile-up that would set a series of terrifying events in motion, culminating in a supervisor investigating the cause of the conveyor-belt stoppage.

Much to my surprise, I was quite good at stickering. It was work that required a steely focus, while at the same time being essentially brainless. After the motions became instinctive, I found that the task freed up my mind to think many exceedingly interesting and significant thoughts, mainly about food. I took pride in my handiwork: the precise centring of each label on a box an important blow struck against the world's disorder.

I started to understand why TS Eliot insisted on continuing to work as a bank clerk even after being offered the funds to give up the job, describing it as 'peaceful'.

Even today, ostensibly pursuing my dream occupation as a writer, I sometimes feel a twinge of nostalgia for that factory assembly line, and the satisfaction of a neatly labelled box. Sometimes when I buy a punnet of supermarket strawberries I run my fingers over its 2-for-1 sticker and pay silent tribute to the human or machine who affixed it there with such noble precision. Then I take those strawberries home and I *wash the hell out of them*.

I wash the hell out of them because at least once an hour, a bottleneck on our assembly line would cause a box of fruit to tip over the conveyor belt and scatter in all directions all over the grimy factory floor. And when that happened, we would scoop those errant berries up and deposit the little fuckers straight back in the box. Together with any dirt, fluff or unidentifiable substances they had inevitably acquired en route.

Obviously we factory workers wouldn't eat them after that. You did, and you still do.

2

Women, Fire and Dangerous Things

In the Australian indigenous language Dyirbal, nouns are divided into separate classes based on cultural associations. One category includes women, fire, and what linguist George Lakoff, in 1987, collectively termed 'dangerous things': snakes, scorpions, spears and so on.

I love that Dyirbal classes women, fire and dangerous things together. It makes me want to learn Dyirbal simply because of that, although it's not the most useful language to spend your time on – there are thought to be less than 30 native speakers in the world. On the plus side, if you and a close friend both learnt Dyirbal, this would make it the perfect secret language to use to bitch about other people in social settings.

The reason I love that Dyirbal groups women with fire and dangerous things is because it flies in the face of prevailing social assumptions about women: that they are weak, docile and essentially non-threatening.

The most absurd evidence I've found of this in recent years was a 2014 study about hurricanes, published in the *Proceedings of the National Academy of Sciences*.

'Hurricanes with Female Names Kill More People,' announced a flurry of headlines.

'Well, that seems weird,' most rational readers presumably responded. 'Why would that be the case?'

In fact, a more accurate headline would have been: 'Deeply Ingrained Sexist Assumptions Can Kill'.

What the study suggested was that if hurricanes have female names, people do not consider them to be as dangerous. As a result, they don't take the same precautions that they would have if the hurricanes were named after men. Of the hurricanes they studied, female-named storms killed almost double the number that male-named storms did.

Because this finding seems almost too ridiculous to be possible, the researchers carried out experiments to test it. When they presented subjects with scenarios involving female hurricanes and male hurricanes, people assumed that the male hurricanes would be more intense. They were less likely to say they'd seek shelter when a female-named hurricane was on the horizon.

'[Our] model suggests that changing a severe hurricane's name from Charley ... to Eloise ... could nearly triple its death toll,' the study commented.

Can we just take a moment to think about that? *People respect hurricanes less if they have a female name.*

'Hurricane Louise is on its way, huh?' people apparently think. 'What's she gonna do, slap me with her handbag?'

And then they die.

Hurricanes were originally *only* named after women. For 26 years, between 1953 and 1979, all hurricanes had female names. In the 1960s, however, feminists started thinking that there was something a little off about this. One of the most vocal campaigners against the practice was a Miami woman called Roxcy Bolton.

I found a clipping from the 20 April 1972 edition of the *Herald-Journal*, which mentions Bolton's endeavours.

'Hurricanes Get Female Names Again', runs the headline. 'The National Hurricane Centre has released 14 feminine names for this season's storms, and a woman immediately sent up gale warnings.' (Get it? Hyuk, hyuk.)

Bolton argued that only naming hurricanes after women was a 'slur', given the destruction wreaked by hurricanes on communities. She suggested that perhaps the Hurricane Center consider naming hurricanes after senators instead, but was told that senators would be insulted. Bolton had a second proposal: name hurricanes after birds.

'But I was told the National Aubudon Society would be up in arms,' Bolton told the *Herald-Journal*. 'Apparently Weather Service officials feel you can't slander senators or birds, but it's all right to run down women.'

Pressure from the likes of Bolton and others eventually saw an end to exclusively female names being given to hurricanes. The practice of alternating between female and male names for hurricanes was introduced in 1979. Bolton did not succeed, however, in another delightful proposal: that the word 'hurricane' be replaced with the word 'him-icane', so it didn't sound so much like 'her-icane'.

I'm a bit conflicted here. On the one hand, I think Bolton was dead right to say that it was sexist *only* to name hurricanes after women, given that there was absolutely no earthly reason for doing so, and knowing that hurricanes are nasty pieces of work. On the other hand, I don't think it would do any harm if an acknowledgement of potential female force was inscribed in language more, the way it is in Dyirbal.

The assumption that women are non-threatening goes way beyond responses to hurricanes. We see its flipside in the fascination with female criminals, for instance.

Some evenings it seems as if the only thing on DSTV are shows about female criminals. 'Women Who Kill'. 'Deadly Women'. 'When Women Kill'. 'Women Behind Bars'. 'Wives With Knives'. I see no evidence of a corresponding volume of television dedicated to profiling male criminality, unless you count the nightly news bulletin. There isn't a TV show called 'When Men Kill', or 'Sons with Guns', or 'Dudes and their Feuds'.

One of the obvious reasons why women who kill are often considered more interesting than men who kill is because men are doing it all the time. That, my friends, is a simple fact. Between 1980 and 2008, men committed 90% of the homicides in the United States. The same rate seems to hold true for most countries. In South Africa, as of 2014, only 2% of sentenced prisoners were female.

(Men's rights activists often point out, as if this makes it better, that men are also overwhelmingly the *victims* of homicide. That is true, and I'm sorry about that, but maybe you dudes could just stop offing each other? Over the centuries women have evolved more sophisticated conflict-management skills, such as calling each other fat.)

So in a way it's natural that women would be perceived as less threatening because, generally speaking, they are. Our responses to violent women suggest something deeper: a fundamental sense that women aren't *supposed* to be dangerous. One of the dominant responses to the White Widow – terror-accused Samantha Lewthwaite – has been sheer incredulity. Partly this is obviously because she is white, as her nickname helpfully draws attention to. But it is also because she is a woman.

In reality there are apparently more women involved in terrorist cells than you might be led to believe by reading most media reports. *Discovery* recently pointed out that since the Chechnya independence movement began using suicide bombers in the early 2000s, more than half of the attacks there have been carried out by women. Indeed, women are allegedly super useful to terrorist movements because they're better able to get past security checkpoints without being challenged.

Women in terrorist organisations are often framed as being manipulated or coerced by male terrorists. The underlying assumption is that it's impossible that women could just want to kill in the name of ideology in exactly the same way men do.

But actually some of them do. Terrorism expert Mia Bloom wrote a book called *Bombshell: The Many Faces of Female Terrorists* in 2011 in which she examined female motivations for participating in terror activities. She found that there were five main reasons: revenge, redemption, relationship, respect and rape.

'I'd really rather be hugging a kitten, but a man told me to wear this scary explosive vest' was not one of them. The women Bloom spoke to within the Irish Republican Army, for instance, said there wasn't a sniff of coercion behind their involvement. They were *enthusiastic*.

Social reluctance to see women as threatening might seem, on one level, quite flattering. It might seem a tacit acceptance that women are less brutish, more respectful of human life, even *less evil*.

But when you scratch the surface, what underpins these attitudes is something rather less complimentary.

Consider the case of Solange Knowles, better known as 'Beyonce's sister'. In May 2014, CCTV footage was released of Solange attacking her brother-in-law, better known as Jay Z, in a lift.

The overwhelming response was hilarity. The internet was instantly a-roar with LOLs. Now, many people pointed out that this reflected an obvious double standard: if Jay Z had been filmed hitting Solange, rather than the other way round, the incident would have attracted outrage.

What this suggests to me, though, is not the extent to which the Feminist Illuminati have succeeded in imposing their agenda upon the world. To me, that a woman hitting a man could be greeted with tears of laughter speaks volumes about perceptions of female powerlessness. It is exactly the same category of response as that old movie chestnut, 'You're so cute when you're angry.'

Of course, I'm not endorsing violence. Violence is wrong and it would be great if men could be less violent, like women. But one thing men have managed to do really well over generations is legitimise their anger. Angry men are feared. They are sometimes hated, but they are also often respected. Angry women, such as Solange Knowles, are often laughed at.

Angry women frequently have to take that anger and turn it into something more socially palatable. I get angry with wearying regularity, but experience has taught me that I have a better chance of being heard if I coat that anger in humour. I have endless respect for women who don't take that route, who express their anger plainly as anger and risk being infantilised – 'Calm down, dear' – or dismissed as hysterical and shrill.

Disapproval of female anger is a great way of stopping women expressing anger in the first place. 'The truth will set you free, but first it will piss you off,' said pioneering feminist Gloria Steinem. 'Empowering' women shouldn't only be about dressing them in shoulder pads and sending them off to job interviews. It should also be about allowing them to express anger without being laughed at.

And if that leads to women being seen as a little more threatening, I'm all for it. Women, fire and dangerous things. Hear us roar.

3

The Perils of Being a
Best White

I was bartending at a remote hotel in the Scottish Highlands once when I served a Scot who was intrigued to learn where I came from. As he got drunker, he insisted on ordering beers in his finest parody of a white South African accent. When he finally slapped down his money to pay and leave, he leant forward and said, meaningfully: 'Thanks, hey ... *kaffir*!'

Then he drunkenly sauntered out, leaving me frozen with horror.

I spent hours agonising over that interaction. Was he just confused about the meaning of 'kaffir'? Did he think it was some cheerful term of endearment employed by South Africans generally, equivalent to how the Brits use 'mate'? Did he imagine South Africans of all stripes walking into a bar and greeting each other with a jovial 'Howzit, kaffir'?

I don't think so. Neither do I believe that he intended it in the Arabic sense of 'infidel', before anyone helpfully suggests that. I imagine that he learnt the word from white South Africans overseas, since it's not a very well-known epithet beyond our borders.

Of course, if he was aware of the meaning of the word, it was bizarre that he would address me with it as a white person. Then again, this was the Scottish Highlands. It wasn't as if there were any black people around to use it on. It is no exaggeration to say that some of the locals – who eked out meagre livings as fishermen or small-scale farmers – had encountered black people only a few times in their lives.

The last time a black person had been seen in the village was more than five years before. It was a visit that was the stuff of legend because the local alcoholic, Darren, had merrily asked him when he intended to wash his face.

Rather than trying to make a cutting point to the racist white South African serving up his drinks, I think my drunken bar patron used 'kaffir' as a farewell salutation because he was clumsily trying to signal some form of racist comradeship with me. A kind of covert solidarity: that he knew the in-language of my people and shared its values.

Sometimes perspective is best attained at a distance. And the results of seeing yourself as the world sees you frequently aren't pretty.

Then again, the rest of the world often doesn't have a leg to stand on. That drunk dude *liked* his assumption that I was a racist, white South African. I've heard of white South Africans travelling overseas during apartheid, and being taken aside by people who whispered something along the lines of: 'Good job there, what you're doing back home. Keep it up.'

While there were many people overseas who firmly supported the anti-apartheid movement, there were also tons who thought apartheid sounded like a pretty solid plan. We know now from released FBI cables that when Nelson Mandela first toured the United States after his release from prison, there were death threats phoned in to every city he visited. And not all of them were made by South Africans phoning long-distance from a crackly tickey-box.

But for sections of the international community who are not diehard racists, the descriptor 'white South African' does not, realistically speaking, always glow with feel-good vibes. Even with all the white South Africans who supported apartheid miraculously having disappeared overnight 20 years ago, as if the Rapture happened in 1994 and it turned out God only really liked racists.

Notwithstanding my drunk Scottish barfly, it is my experience that when people hear 'I am a white South African', their automatic impulse is often *not* to clap you on the shoulder and hand you a foamy beer, the way they might if you'd said 'I am a bobsledding Jamaican'.

To many sections of the local and global population, 'white South African' is still synonymous with cartoonish evil and a penchant for khaki: sepia TV footage of heavily moustached men in too-short shorts barking orders at downtrodden black people.

Like it or not, the lingering reputation of white South Africans is not 'hardworking people who pay their taxes and are quite good at swimming'. It is 'people who created and sustained a society that systematically stripped black people of their personhood'.

Is this fair?

These days there is a growing resentment among young, white South Africans who have been lumped into this unflattering tribe. They remain on the wrong side of a history they weren't even alive for. It wasn't *them* who did all those horrible things to blacks.

It wasn't *me*, for God's sake. I never asked a black person for their pass book, or stripped them of property rights, or herded them into Bantustans, or even voted for the people who did do that stuff. Other than visibly and magnificently prospering from a political system that oppressed them for centuries, the most demeaning thing I have knowingly done to a black person is force my friend Osiame to dance with me after too much wine at a dinner party.

But the pesky thing about history is that you can't just take it off and hang it up like a coat.

Most white South Africans have jobs. Their unemployment rate is around 5%. That is *sweet*. That's like Iceland, which only has about 500 000 people in it to start with. It is as if Oprah made white South Africa and put a job under 95% of the studio audience's seats. *You* get a job and *you* get a job and *you* get a job!

And when you get that job, on average you're paid higher than pretty much anyone else in the country – four times higher, according to recent statistics. You're more likely to be well educated. You'll live longer. If you are born a white South African, by virtually every standard internationally, you are winning in life's lottery.

That's the plus side of being a white South African.

The down side is that you walk around carrying the burden of being one of history's baddies on your back. And sometimes it feels crushing, but then you can always go for a swim in your giant money-pool to console yourself. We're like cautionary characters in a fairy tale with a sledgehammer moral about trading your soul for gold.

I don't personally have any gold, I should clarify, just so nobody wastes time with me when the revolution comes. You should go straight to number 15 in my block of flats, because I think they have some Le Creuset casserole dishes. I'm not rich at all and neither are a lot of the white South Africans I know. We're only rich when compared with most of the South African population, which isn't a currency you can buy salmon with at Woolies.

But the reason we're richer isn't because we're more clever and more hard working. It's because for centuries people who looked like us oppressed the hell out of people who didn't look like us. We've never had to compete on a level playing field, and we still don't, because we're still dragging apartheid behind us like a zombie corpse.

Legendary investor Warren Buffett said that one of the reasons for his success was that he only had to compete against half the population. He meant that for much of his career, women's entry into business was either formally or informally blocked. White South Africans have only had to compete against 8% of the population for a significant portion of their history.

Whenever white South Africans express unease about this state of affairs on an online platform, there is *always* a white person in the comments who sneers: 'Well if you feel so bad about it, you should quit your job so that a black person can have it.'

I can never think of a good response to that because despite the fact that the commenter is self-evidently a mega-twat, part of me thinks they might be right. I don't want to give up my job, obviously – partly because I think I'm quite good at it and mainly because I'm not constitutionally cut out for a life on the street. I would definitely develop a galloping tik addiction within days.

Speaking frankly, I also don't see why I should have to be the one to give up my job. If we're going to make a list, surely it should be topped by all the ex-National Party politicians who somehow became ANC members of parliament during the transition to democracy while the rest of us were distracted with not killing each other?

What, then, is one to do? The philosopher Samantha Vice took a stab at this thorny question a few years ago, and her suggestion – which I am grotesquely over-simplifying – was essentially that white people in South Africa should 'cultivate humility and silence'. I see the merits of this, I really do, but as someone who is quite chatty I struggle with it.

Then Desmond Tutu really set the cat among the pigeons by proposing that white South Africans should pay a 'white tax', to which many white people responded with fury that they already paid a 'white tax' called 'tax'.

It's cute how many white people genuinely believe they are the only ones who pay tax, as if whenever anyone else gets to the Shoprite till, the checkout lady presses a secret button marked 'NO VAT FOR DARKIES'.

The way a lot of young white South Africans I know deal with their existential plight, other than by drinking heavily, is by becoming Best Whites.

Everyone knows a Best White. Here is a short field guide to spotting one in the wild.

1) Best Whites are in an imaginary competition with everyone else in their blighted race. The competition is, in crude terms, a kind of anti-racism pageant. If you win it, when you arrive at the Pearly Gates and are greeted by a black God, She will say: 'Congratulations. All those other whites were quite racist, but *you* are the very opposite of racist.'

2) Best Whites compete aggressively to spot and publically denounce white racism. Best Whites prefer the most racist possible interpretation of other white people's words, so their racism detectors are perpetually pinging.

3) Best Whites will initiate a conversation about white privilege within five minutes of meeting a black person in order to firmly establish the ideological gulf that separates them from bad whites.

4) Best Whites may, at one stage or another, have flirted with an Africa tattoo.

5) If the Best White is male, he may exhibit a compulsion to address black males in the service industry as 'brother'.

6) Best Whites will casually mention their parents' Struggle credentials to car guards.

7) Best Whites claim they went to schools that were interracial from the time of Jan van Riebeeck.

It should be understood that there is a vast difference between Best Whites (capitals) and *actual* best whites. In the latter category see: Bram Fischer, Helen Suzman, George Bizos, Beyers Naudé, Johnny Clegg, Neil Tovey.

I have strong Best White tendencies. I'm pretty sure that, on balance, it is better to be a Best White than an outspoken racist, but there is no denying that Best Whites can be exceedingly irritating.

I also suspect that being a Best White is in itself quite racist, because the elaborate performance of anti-racism to black people that it demands is tailored to the race of the hearer. Best Whites operate under the assumption that black people love nothing more than a sympathetic white ear into which they can pour their lived experiences of racism.

In a generation's time, maybe being a Best White will seem as outdated and irrelevant a performance as someone who arrives at work on Rollerblades. Until then, you'll find us checking our privilege. And then checking to make sure everyone's noticed.

4

In Praise of the High Five

One of my most fervent wishes as an adult has been that we could standardise one form of physical greeting. In my ideal society, it would be compulsory for everyone to greet each other with a high five. (This would make it an authoritarian but cheery society, perhaps run along the lines of Willy Wonka's chocolate factory.)

Of course, the compulsory high five could be deviated from under exceptional circumstances – arranged in advance by mutual agreement over email or WhatsApp. Reunion of long-lost friends? Seeing your son off to war? Greeting a lover who just spent a decade in jail for a crime he or she didn't commit? Hug away. Hug it out.

One of the scenarios I have deliberately excluded from a special hug concession is that of 'reunion of siblings separated at birth'. That's because of the quirky little phenomenon known as Genetic Sexual Attraction, in which genetic relatives who meet for the first time as adults immediately want to shag each other's brains out. This is no joke: one study in the UK found that as many as 50% of post-adoption reunions are characterised by 'strong sexual feelings in one or both participants'. Perhaps best to stick to a warm handshake there.

Thousands of hours of my adult life have been spent obsessing in advance about the most appropriate way to greet someone I am about to meet up with. Do we hug? Are we there yet? Do we kiss? Are we kissing friends? Do we, God forbid, kiss each cheek in turn, like people in an Italian ice cream advert?

In my experience, what happens in roughly 75% of situations is that the other participant has resolved to do exactly the opposite of what you have planned for. On the occasions when I go in hard for a kiss on arrival, I invariably end up planting a smooch on the other person's ear-hole, or somewhere in mid-air, since they are hanging over my shoulder with absolutely no kissing intentions. When this occurs, I sometimes compensate by making a loud and theatrical 'mwah' sound to cover the awkwardness, as if this was always my plan. As if forcing kisses on unwilling recipients is a campy affectation I've developed over the years. As if it's my 'thing'.

After this initial misfire, the interaction turns into a fatal psychological tussle of rock-paper-scissors, where you attempt to predict what their farewell gambit will be based on their opening move. But because both parties are playing the same mind game, both of you now do the opposite of what you originally did, due to an entirely illogical belief in the consistency of other people's social behaviour. Now, on parting, the other person is guaranteed to come in lunging for a juicy kiss, only to find you chastely turning your head away like a frigid Jane Austen character.

The issue is further complicated by the range of possible greeting permutations these days. Some young people now like to acknowledge meeting someone *for the first time* with a kiss on the cheek – though no hug. This leaves you two options: either to leave your hands dangling by your sides while you exchange pecks, like someone bobbing for apples at a carnival, or briefly to rest your hand on their shoulder or their hip, which feels like an uncomfortably intimate posture for two people who have already forgotten each other's names.

Don't get me started on people with whom you are not having sexual intercourse who try to greet you with a kiss on the lips. Stop doing this immediately!

Cultural differences add an additionally torturous dimension. Some white South Africans assume that all black South Africans expect to be greeted with a 'comrades' handshake', helpfully defined by one website as follows: 'Start with a firm, full-hand handclasp. Swap once to an inverted handclasp. Back to firm handclasp. All done quickly.'

Initiating the comrades' handshake with every black person in sight, from militant trade unionists to the CEOs of multinational corporations, is another hallmark of the Best White. But it's an understandable safety measure; for a Best White to be caught unawares by a comrade's handshake feels crushing, as if you were so blinded by white supremacy that you never even anticipated the possibility that the palm pressed into yours could be angling for an upwards thrust. You might as well admit to underpaying your domestic worker and move to Orania immediately.

This quagmire of potentially misinterpreted cues is why I am a vocal advocate for the standardising of the high five as a greeting. For a start, high fives are intrinsically jolly. It is nice to be high-fived. There's a reason why high fives make babies laugh till they soil themselves: they are fun. Executed proficiently, they make a satisfying sound: a 'thwack' of joyful camaraderie.

They are the definition of mutuality: they require exactly the same physical action from each party. Nobody leaves a high five feeling that they might have inadvertently exposed some creepy, inner yearning. They demand the bare minimum of physical contact: a millisecond's worth of palm touching palm.

Admittedly, when you start thinking about high fives too intently, they begin to seem a bit weird. This is doubly the case if you read the Wikipedia explanation: 'The high five is a celebratory hand gesture that occurs when two people simultaneously raise one hand each, about head-high, and push, slide, or slap the flat of their palm against the flat palm of the other person. The gesture is often preceded verbally by a phrase like "Give me five" or "High five".'

You can imagine an alien earnestly studying that entry, and then standing in front of a Martian mirror mouthing the words 'Give me five. Give me *five!* Give *me* five!', while swishing a tentacle about head-high.

After extensive scholarly research on Wikipedia, I was amazed to learn that the high five probably only originated in the late 1970s. It seems like such an instinctive action that I'd pictured it as being around since biblical times. Moses parting the Red Sea and being high-fived by every passing Israelite. Lady Macbeth and her husband sharing an unclean 'highe five' after the murder of King Duncan.

Not so. One widely held theory is that the high five was invented by an American baseball player called Glenn Burke, who was playing for the Los Angeles Dodgers one fateful day in 1977.

Team member Dusty Baker had just scored a home run. It was a thrilling moment of celebration. Here's how sports journalist Jon Mooallem describes what happened next: 'Burke, waiting on deck, thrust his hand enthusiastically over his head to greet his friend at the plate. Baker, not knowing what to do, smacked it. "His hand was up in the air, and he was arching way back," says Baker. "So I reached up and hit his hand. It seemed like the thing to do."'

Well, that could have ended differently, couldn't it? What if Baker, in the heat of the moment, had thought that something *else* was 'the thing to do' when confronted with a raised hand? What if he'd simply concluded that the best response was to raise his own hand in the air correspondingly, like two people at a praise and worship session? What if he'd decided that a hilarious thing to do would be to tickle Burke's unguarded armpit? What steely presence of mind, what unerring social instincts, to realise that the *perfect* thing to do would be to slap Burke's palm!

We owe those two men a great debt, though it's normally Burke who gets all the credit. This seems manifestly unfair to me, leaving Baker as the Art Garfunkel of the high five. Before Baker slapped Burke's hand, after all, there *was* no high five. Just a dude with his hand aimlessly hanging in the air.

This poignant image brings me to a problem with the high five that must be acknowledged. The great advantage of the high five – its pure mutuality – is also its potential downfall. There are few social slights as devastating as a shunned high five. The most common way of pretending it hasn't happened – running your hand through your hair as if it were always intended as one fluid motion – is feeble and tragic. It doesn't work. Everyone knows what just happened and they pity you.

A miss-hit high five is a terrible spectacle to behold, too. You'd think directing two hands to make flat contact in the air would be a sure thing for people without severe mental or physical impairments, but things go wrong with stunning regularity. The only possible face-saving option is to loudly demand a do-over: 'C'mon, that wasn't a proper high five!', but you have to be the one to say it first, in order to imply that it's the other person who hasn't gained full mastery of his or her body yet.

But despite the potential for error, the advantages of the high five seem to outweigh the pitfalls. The best part of standardising its use for greetings is that *you'd always know what to do*. There would be none of the excruciating will-we-won't-we tango that too often prefaces a hug. The palm contact of the high five is also too short-lived to be able to draw any weird conclusions about masculinity or character from its texture, as people often do with handshakes.

Until this idea takes off, I have a simple plea: for people to signal clearly their intentions in the moments directly preceding a greeting.

If you intend to hug someone, advance upon them with your arms flung open, perhaps while yelling: 'Hug-plane cleared for landing!' If you aspire to a cheek peck, walk up with your mouth already dramatically screwed into a kissy pout. If all you want is a handshake, approach with your arm rigidly stuck forward like a bayonet. We'll all be better off, I promise.

5

Love in the Time of Internet: Part I

It's hard to find love, and social media is making *not* finding love substantially harder to deal with. In order to have hundreds of couples being couply smashed squarely in your face at one time, you used to have to go to a Moonie wedding. Now you simply log on to Facebook and every seemingly irredeemable twat from your high school maths class is making their partner a hashtagged breakfast in bed.

Women, in particular, are bombarded with messages – both tacit and explicit – that settling for practically *anyone* is better than being single.

'He's in jail, you say? For a killing spree? He's got lovely eyes, hey. Lucky girl.'

This isn't even a joke. Convicted criminals have to practically beat off women with bats, which may ironically be what got them behind bars in the first place. I recently finished reading the prison memoir of South African drug mule Shani Krebs, in which he records two-timing a veritable harem of women while languishing in a Bangkok jail for over two decades. The man was taking showers in open sewerage and women simply could not get enough of that goodness. Oscar Pistorius literally pumped four bullets into a human female and allegedly had a new girlfriend before the year was out. Tabloids reported that her father was chuffed to bits with the match.

In June 2014, police in Stockton, California, posted a picture of a convicted felon called Jeremy Meeks on the station's Facebook page. Meeks had been arrested on weapons charges as part of a high-level police crackdown on shootings and robberies. He also happened to be flipping gorgeous. His picture attracted more than 50 000 Facebook 'likes' within a day. 'Omg that face structure … those eyes … that skin tone,' rhapsodised one fan. 'You get one call in prison right? CALL ME JEREMY,' urgently exhorted another. Donations towards his bail poured in.

Some commentators expressed bemusement that a man who, apart from anything else, had a tattoo of a teardrop – which is often taken to mean that the wearer has killed someone – was attracting immodest proposals from thousands of internet women. One Facebook user earnestly interpreted: 'Their drooling bcuz most ppl don't see an issue with a good-looking man carrying weapons whether they are legal or illegal. I am not saying it is my opinion actually mine is quite the opposite I believe in legally purchasing weapons regardless of ones looks.'

Someone give that lady a judgeship.

Just so we're all on the same page, Jeremy Meeks was described by police as 'one of the most violent criminals in the Stockton area'. But apparently the Bible had it right: the Meeks shall inherit the Earth.

There are three potential morals to this little tale. The first is obviously the enduring appeal of the 'bad boy' throughout history (see: Henry VIII, Charles Manson, Kenny Kunene). The second is that women can be every bit as shallow and appearance-focused as men in their choice of mates. But the third moral of the story is that it seems there is very little a man can do to definitively rule himself out as a bit of a catch.

Social discomfort with single women is a phenomenon that seems to sweep across all known cultural lines. There might be some tribe in the Amazon where all the women swagger around single and everyone high fives them, but I've yet to read about it. My Greek friend Cristina attracted an enormous amount of concern, prior to finding a boyfriend, for being the oldest spinster in her Peloponnese village. She was 24.

The most irritating thing about being single, other than the entire universe of social media, is the amount of unsolicited well-meaning advice you get from smugly coupled friends. The American comic Maria Bamford mimics this discourse effectively in one of her stand-up routines in a droning, sing-song tone: 'Just stop looking. The minute you stop looking, that special someone will walk into your life.'

This is totally shit advice, essentially advocating a stance of fatalistic paralysis. Nobody would ever give you the same counsel about job hunting. 'Just stop looking. The minute you stop looking, that special, high-paying, managerial role with great medical aid will fall into your lap.'

Fortunately, most of the single men and women I know have adopted a decidedly proactive approach towards relationship seeking. Sometimes it works, sometimes it doesn't. And sometimes people are confused about what they want.

As an illustration of the latter point, I once phoned a number that my friend Kirby found scrawled on the wall of a public toilet. 'Looking 4 sex phone [cellphone number]', the message read. I wasn't actually in the market for sex with the type of person who advertises his or her hunger for coitus in shaky koki on a wall, but we thought it would be an interesting anthropological experiment to see what resulted. Either that or I'd lost a bet.

So I called the number. A man answered after a few rings.

'Yes, hello, I'm looking for sex,' I announced smoothly.

'Uh ... sorry?' he said, after a slight pause.

'Your number. It was written in the Tstitsikamma Engen toilet? To call for sex?' I clarified, with increasing awkwardness. Only then did the thought occur to me that perhaps one of his shithead friends had penned it there for giggles. But that wasn't the case.

'Ja, okay,' he said – in, I was slightly hurt to note, a somewhat unenthusiastic tone. 'Uh ... where are you?'

He explained that he lived in a city about 200 kilometres from the toilet. But, he said, he would be travelling that way again the following Tuesday, if I'd care to meet up then.

'That would be lovely,' I said, and hung up abruptly because I was about to laugh loudly into the phone.

Discussing the interaction in detail for several hours afterwards, Kirby and I agreed that the most mysterious element of this stranger's casual contracting to a tryst with me was that he had left his number in a *men's toilet*. Was he just ... exceptionally sexually liberated? Was 'any hole a goal', as the poets have it? Or do I sound like a big, beefy hunk of manhood over the phone?

While a student in the UK, I contemplated taking a job as a phone-sex operator. I couldn't think of many other jobs I could do while lying horizontal – other than the obvious, of course, which I was absolutely *not* up for. The phone-sex business seemed like money for jam, to be frank. I wouldn't even have to make any dirty stuff up. My potential employers said they'd give me a script to read and all I'd have to do was rattle it off. I never got to see the actual script, but I'd already read some sociolinguistic studies on the language of phone-sex operators, so I was familiar with the general vibe.

A lot of what's required is tedious detail about the fabric and colour of the imaginary garment you hypothetically have on. 'I'm wearing a ... peach ... silk ... negligee,' you'd aspirate huskily, while wiping bits of pizza cheese off your soiled hoodie.

I didn't take the job in the end only because they wanted to photocopy my passport and I was scared the university would find out and expel me.

I don't know anyone who admits to being a regular user of anonymous phone-sex services, but I do know a ton of people who are turning to technology to find love and sex, in the form of internet dating sites. This seems perfectly sensible to me, since it's the only pairing mechanism in human history that lets you vet potential partners for spelling and grammar problems before you sleep with them. Unless you're a predatory English teacher, in which case I hope you're reading this in the prison library.

A lot of people think internet dating is intrinsically shameful, as if embarking down this road is an admission that you have the social skills of a cabbage. The logic is completely off, since if *you're* nice and normal and turning to the internet for matchmaking help, chances are that there are loads of other nice and normal people in the same boat. It feels *passé* even to be giving an endorsement of internet dating, since it's now been around for so long that people who met online and got married are already getting divorced.

If you ask me if I think you should start internet dating, I'll say 'Go for it, babes', and slug back my drink with a thousand-yard stare. I'm conflicted, you see, because on the one hand many of my friends have found enduring, storybook love on dating sites. On the other hand, I can tell you from personal experience that there is a *gigantic con* at the heart of at least some dating sites.

This is my story. You'll need to turn the page …

6

Love in the Time of Internet: Part 2

'Start internet dating,' they tell you. 'Everyone's doing it!' And indeed they are. It is the romantic modus operandi of the zeitgeist. Except that it turns out that not everyone in the zeitgeist is a real live humanoid.

Back in the summer of 2007, when I was living and studying in the UK, I started working for an extremely successful company that ran multiple internet dating sites. I was taken on in an unspecified role, but I assumed the work would involve some basic admin. 'Doing admin' was essentially the realisation of all my wildest career dreams, since it involved neither a hairnet nor asking bar patrons to please stop 'interfering with themselves' in the downstairs toilet.

'Admin' was my golden ticket to the status of a white-collar worker. I overlooked the fact that I was absolutely hopeless at any personal administrative tasks and focused on what I saw as the tremendous perks of this mode of employment. Drinking coffee from a ceramic mug. Sitting on my very own chair. Possible access to stationery. Not wearing a humiliating uniform. There might be biscuits.

It seems like a low bar now, but at the time I felt like I'd been head-hunted to be the CEO of Google. Until I got home after my first day on the job and had to pour myself an enormous glass of WTF. You see, the coffee, the chair and the stationery were all present and accounted for, though there was a troubling scarcity of biscuits. It was the actual *job* that turned out to be a wee bit of a problem.

It was essential to the business's success that users of the dating sites sent messages to other users because the only way of sending return mes-sages was to become a 'full' member and pay a monthly subscription fee. But in the cruel economy of internet dating, not everyone gets messaged. Some are deemed too unattractive. Some have rubbish profiles. Others don't put up any photos, which automatically lowers their chance of at-tracting messages.

These people are no-hopers. You're running a business – you can't just sit back and leave it to Cupid that someone will message them because Cupid is an unreliable little creep. You've got to take that shit into your own hands.

Enter the 'pseudos'. That was the internal term used for what normal people would call 'fake dating profiles'.

Our task was to create these false profiles and release them into the system. Nothing was random; there was a highly organised system under-pinning it all. An online spreadsheet would tell you each day the basics of who you were supposed to be: woman or man, age range, location. It was your job to flesh out the details of this imaginary human: a name, an oc-cupation, a back-story, hobbies and interests.

On my first day, I was assigned a pseudo that had already been created by one of my co-workers. Her name was Maxine. She was 37, unmarried, an interior designer running her own small business. Maxine was extremely attractive, but I was to learn that this wasn't usually the case. To avoid suspicion, we'd generally use photos of average-looking people. You know, the type of person who might plausibly send you a message on an internet dating site.

'Where do you get the photos?' I asked my neighbour.

'Random MySpace profiles,' she replied matter-of-factly. There was a system for that, too. The spreadsheet specified which nationality's MySpace profiles you should plunder on any particular day. They favoured slightly obscure European countries, such as Macedonia.

Once you'd fleshed out your pseudo's profile, and given him or her the face of some unsuspecting Macedonian, you'd send out a generic flirty message to about 5 000 users of the dating site at once. Nothing elaborate or too clever. 'Hey hun, fancy a chat? x.' That was pretty much ideal.

And then you'd wait for the messages to flood the pseudo's inbox.

My task, now, was to *become* Maxine. To respond individually to hundreds of messages in the manner of a 37-year-old interior designer from Wiltshire looking for love. Judging by the profile my co-worker had created, Maxine was pretty sloppy on the spelling and punctuation front. Maxine also sounded like a bit of a drip, and potentially a lush – the first line of her profile read: 'Its only after a couple of glasses of vino that I have been able to pluck up the couradge and give this a go.'

It sucked pretty hard that Maxine was an interior designer, since men kept pressing me for details of my tastes in decor, which in real life amount to 'placing a rug wherever the most obvious red wine stains are'.

I stuck to distinctly broad brushstrokes. 'Love a good lamp,' I'd write airily. 'Lighting can really make or break a room if u kno what I mean'.

That stuff was easier than the specifics, which really ate up time. One man told Maxine the first single he'd ever bought was some Roxy Music song, and then asked her what the first single *she* ever purchased was. I had to calculate at what age 37-year-old Maxine would've started forking out for music. I decided she bought her first album in 1980, when she was 10 years old. Then I had to Google 1980s chart-topping hits to find Maxine's favourite. I settled on Dolly Parton's '9-to-5', though in retrospect I think that was a weird choice for 10-year-old Maxine. If I had another shot at it I'd go with Blondie's 'Call Me'.

Worse was to come. The second pseudo I tackled had also been pre-created by a co-worker. In this case, Sharon was a 43-year-old single mother of two, who had sadistically specified in her profile that the two things she enjoyed most in life were 'kicking the leaves in autumn and hearing my children laugh uncontrollably over something we've done together'. Sharon could spell and write in full sentences, but she also had to bang on about her hyper-amused kids the whole bloody time.

You'd normally exchange about three messages before the correspondents started hinting about meeting up. Then you'd have to pull the plug. My standard line was to explain that I'd met up with someone from the site the night before and it had gone really well. Then I'd add a softener: 'Good luck with your journey hun x.' Not since the Second World War spy cables had the word 'hun' appeared so often in textual form.

Because the firm's human resources department seemed to have classified me as either 'classy' or 'a bit of a prude', I didn't have to do any 'adult' messaging. This wasn't the case for most of my co-workers, who had to alternate between vanilla sites and the XXX stuff. There was a spreadsheet for that, too, assigning workers to niche areas of sexual interest.

'Who's on anal? Mel, you on anal?' they'd yell across the office in the morning. My co-workers were universally young, blonde and gorgeous. ('They cost the same as the ugly ones,' the boss once cracked.) If only the male clients of the sites knew that the real-life women they were corresponding with – myself excepted – were far more attractive than the personae they adopted online, I sometimes mused.

I didn't have much time for musing, though, because I was too busy being seized with guilt and shame about my line of work. The company had an official spiel in defence of the 'pseudo' practice. They claimed the trick was merely to boost their clients' confidence so they started messaging real people. Or, as the boss put it unofficially: 'If you're some lonely fat old bloke who gets a message from a fit young bird to brighten up your day, isn't that better than no one messaging you at all?'

I wasn't convinced. Some of the messages my pseudos received were soaked in such profound loneliness that they haunted me for weeks. A further problem was that I found it hard to shrug off my day's false identities when I got home each night. I'd lie in bed wondering what DVD Sharon's kids were nagging her to buy, or trying to decide where Maxine was taking her summer holiday this year. Suzie, Tamara, Simon, Jayne, Mark ...

I imagine that's what fiction authors go through while they're writing a novel, except fiction authors can probably maintain firm eye contact with themselves in a mirror.

But I can't lie: it was also *fascinating*. I existed in a constant state of helpless giggles, horror and awe. I honestly could not believe the kind of stuff that people deemed appropriate for enticing online courtship. I started keeping a running highlights log.

A bit about me, one correspondent casually began his message. *In the early 1970s I was arrested and subsequently convicted of murder. After serving 27 years I had my conviction quashed in the Court of Appeal in 2001.* I suppose that *is* the kind of thing you'd want to get off your chest pretty sharpish, but it seems like a high-risk opening gambit.

Some of my online boyfriends had profoundly unsexy jobs. *I make parts for inside your body, like hip, knee, elbow, joints etc*, one announced. Another confessed: *Most people think funeral directors are vey solom, not so when we go out for a night out we let are hair down and realy enjoy life ironical i know but we have to do it.* And good for you, Mr Death.

I admired those with extremely precise ideas about what they were looking for. *My ideal partner would be in similar health as myself, slender, have teeth and hair but not nostral or hair growing from ears.* A pragmatic and attainable checklist.

This, not so much: *I also like a woman with good dress sense and looks after her appearance, all glammed up on a Saturday night but also looks great in ripped jeans, a worn t-shirt and muddy wellies. Someone who if out walking and saw a rope swing over a stream, just wouldn't be able to resist it. A woman who enjoys a snowball fight, someone who, while I'm up the stepladder painting the ceiling, she is painting the backs of my heals, just for devilment.*

Let's be frank about it: what you are looking for is a 12-year-old boy.

Folksy sexism seemed to be the language of love for some of my pen pals. *I prefer a good action film, some soppy ones are all right but usually a woman in a good film spoils it, slows the action down, and that's my only bit if male chauvanism, I think!!! OOPS! I can hear you now 'the pig'. Sorry, got to be honest.* No sweat, piggy!

So you like to paint … my house needs a lick of paint … sorry only joking have to say sorry because i know how sensitive you arty lady types are. Yes, sensitive like Valerie Solanas.

One bloke had clearly missed his calling as a motivational speaker. *Why not go for your goal babe you are pretty and still have all the world and all your life before you*, he wrote. *Go for it Hun and never let anyone put you down, I also need a secretary in my Bolton office.*

THIS IS WHY YOU'RE SINGLE raged part of me, while the other part wondered if being a secretary in his Bolton office would be better than being his fake online girlfriend.

I liked the ones that left me with unanswered questions. *First of all my names Darren (long story).* How? If your name was 'Excalibur', or 'Goebbels', it might warrant a long story. How can it possibly be a 'long story' that your name is *Darren*? Just how boring would that long story be?

My father had a blood disorder that made him resistant 2 cold, and he passed that resistance down in smaller measures. Is this your way of telling me that you are half lizard?

By the way your skin looks very comfortable, what do you wear when you take it off? Nice try, Hannibal Lecter.

I became adept in the vocabulary of a married man seeking an affair.

I still live with my wife and 2 children. But the relationship is doomed.

My marriage is I'm afraid to say in a terminal state of decay and we are talking about separating.

My 'ex' has just gone to bed so I won't be disturbed! She doesn't know about this site yet. We have decided to divorce, though living together for a while.

I am looking for a female friend away from my 'normal' life.

These messages made me sad. I hoped their wives were secretly having it off with the neighbour, though I recognised I was in a poor position to take the moral high ground.

Five years after I worked there, two of the company's previous employees blew the whistle on the 'pseudo' practice in a Channel Four exposé. By then they said they'd stopped doing it, though I wasn't convinced because it seemed such an integral part of the business model.

Nowadays, when friends tell me they're internet dating, I wish them all the best and tell them to watch out for anyone who looks faintly Macedonian. Late at night, I sometimes wonder what happened to my online dating pen pals. Did they find love with an actual human being? Do they ever think of Maxine? And if you were to harness the energy of the world's loneliness, could it power every major city on the globe?

7

Kindles and the Future of Reading

When Kindles came out, one of the reasons why everyone got so **excited was because they enabled you to read shameful books in public without other people knowing. Gone were the days of concealing your copy of *Harry Potter* beneath the dust jacket of *War and Peace*. Kindles promised to keep your literary secrets.**

I can sort of understand this aspect of their appeal, though the only book I have ever felt genuinely ashamed about buying in hard copy was *Fifty Shades of Grey*. I bought it only a day after it had come out in South Africa, which made it extra embarrassing, as if I'd set an alert on my phone to ensure I got in before the masses on this milestone of pornographic publishing. The early bird catches the wank, and all that.

Of course, the man selling it to me couldn't let its purchase go by without comment, even though you'd think bookstores would give special training to their staff to maintain a noble silence in these precise scenarios. When ringing up a book like *Fifty Shades of Grey*, a flashing red reminder should pop up on their screens: SAY NOTHING, GIGGLE AFTER.

On this occasion, the bookseller had clearly missed his discretion training. He looked at me conspiratorially as I handed him my copy over the desk.

'I believe that's a bit of a *rowwe* [rough] one,' he said.

What's the appropriate response to that, anyway? 'Rough's the way I like 'em, big boy!' with a creepy wink?

'I'm reading it for work,' I snapped defensively instead. Which was absolutely true, but had the disadvantage of sounding like an obvious lie because what kind of 'work' requires you to read soft porn? (I have suddenly thought of multiple answers to this, including 'the work done by someone who buys up the options on soft porn novels to turn them into soft porn movies', but the point still basically stands.) I would have been happy to circumvent that exchange by purchasing *Fifty Shades of Grey* as an e-book for Kindle, but I didn't have one at the time.

I would also have found it embarrassing to read *Fifty Shades of Grey* in hard copy in public. I could pretend this is because of the abysmal quality of the writing, but really it's just because it's all about sex and I'd be scared that I'd be inadvertently wriggling around in my seat and biting my bottom lip in visible arousal.

There are other books that I'd rather read on Kindle than have to display their covers to the world. Joseph Conrad's *The Nigger of the Narcissus* is a prime example. If you are going to whip that shit out in public, you had better be damn sure that everyone within spitting distance is well acquainted with early Modernist literature, because otherwise you will be assumed to be a Grand Wizard of the Ku Klux Klan.

Self-help books are also quite embarrassing to read in public. If you saw someone deeply absorbed in *He's Just Not That Into You*, would your immediate response be: (a) 'How wonderful to see such introspection and reflectiveness in action'; or (b) 'Shame man'? I put it to you that it would be (b).

Having said that, the punchiness of some self-help titles make them almost irresistibly alluring. I haven't read *If You Want Closure In Your Relationship Start With Your Legs*, but I'm tempted to – even though the title does appear to give away the crux of the advice gratis.

Other self-help titles seem to solve their own dilemma. Let's take *Men Who Hate Women and the Women Who Love Them: When Loving Hurts and You Don't Know Why*, for instance. Could it be that the riddle posed by the last half of the title is quite compellingly answered by everything before the colon?

That is definitely a book that you'd have to buy on Kindle if you were planning to read it on holiday with your husband.

'What's that you're reading there, honey?'

'Oh, just *Men Who Hate Women and the Women Who Love Them*. Please pass the sunscreen.'

In general, though, I'm a firm advocate of the idea that reading practically *anything* is better than reading nothing. There are some exceptions, obviously, such as *Mein Kampf* if you're reading it as an intriguing how-to guide rather than as an exposition of insane bigotry. Or the Al-Qaeda magazine, mainly because you can be arrested in certain countries simply for possessing it – even though it goes by the slightly hilarious title *Inspire*, as if it were published by Oprah.

I always find it fascinating to see what people do read. One of the reasons I feel anxious about the increasing use of e-readers like Kindles is because then we won't have an easy way of making snap judgements about people based on their taste in books. Who knows what you're hiding inside that Kindle? The collected works of Paulo Coehlo? Ayn Rand? *If You Want Closure In Your Relationship Start With Your Legs*?

It's also considered perfectly socially acceptable to intently scrutinise someone's bookshelf. Indeed, that's half the reason most of us cultivate bookshelves in the first place: in the hope that someone will see our impressive books and decide to have sex with us immediately. I feel like Kindle etiquette would work distinctly differently, though. Grabbing someone's Kindle off a table and saying 'Let's have a look at what's in this thing, then', seems like an aggressive violation of privacy.

One of the good things about Kindles, though, is that they're offering us new insights into how people read. An example is the 'highlighting' feature. When people read books on Kindle, they can digitally highlight passages they find significant or powerful as they go along. Unless you turn this feature off, you can see the most highlighted passages while you read, which is either irritating or helpful, depending on your perspective. (Do you like it when you borrow a book from the library and someone's underlined all their favourite bits? That's essentially what this is, but based on consensus from thousands of readers.)

This is interesting for two reasons. The first is simply to see what people find worthy of highlighting. It's often not what you'd think. One of the most highlighted sentences in *Fifty Shades of Grey* is: 'The growth and development of people is the highest calling of leadership.' It's not clear how we should respond to the idea that people are apparently reading *Fifty Shades of Grey* as some sort of business manual, but I'm sure it won't end well.

The second reason why the highlighting feature of Kindles is interesting was suggested by the *Wall Street Journal*. That writer of the article pointed out that if people are finishing a book all the way to the end, you'd expect the highlights to be distributed throughout the book. If you're only seeing highlights in the first few chapters, there's a good chance that people are simply giving up on it.

What the uneven dispersal of highlights suggests, for instance, is that almost nobody reads physicist Stephen Hawking's *A Brief History of Time* through to the end, even though it's sold 10 million copies. This is no shocker. People basically buy *A Brief History of Time* in order to display it ostentatiously in their homes as an alternative to getting a massive forehead tattoo saying I AM CLEVER, REALLY.

A more recent example is economist Thomas Piketty's *Capital in the*

Twenty-First Century, another runaway bestseller that it seems virtually nobody is finishing. In fairness, that book is 700 pages long. For that kind of investment, it better give you the meaning of life, including when loving hurts and you don't know why.

You can guarantee that Tolstoy's *War and Peace* is another member of the Rarely Finished club. I once took *War and Peace* along as my only reading material for a five-hour layover at Windhoek's Hoseo Kutako airport, banking on the idea that sheer desperation would eventually force me to get stuck in. I ended up spending four-and-a-half hours staring at the flight information board. In fairness, *War and Peace* is hailed by many people I know as a book that *may* actually give you the meaning of life, so my failure to commit to it should be chalked up to nothing more than feeble-mindedness on my side.

If e-readers do become our dominant mode of reading, though, maybe we'll see books like these drop in sales while others rocket in popularity. If nobody can see what you're buying, you might as well make it the stuff you *actually* want to read, as opposed to the stuff you think you ought to read. It's estimated that over 2 million entirely new books are published worldwide every year – without counting reprints of old books or the increasing numbers of self-published works. When I think about that figure I start to feel panicky, imagining all the gems within them that I'll never discover. Books spilling off shelf after shelf, standing dusty and unloved before being carted off to be pulped, carrying the hopes of their author along to the dump.

It's comforting to think that sometimes books get a second chance at greatness, as was the case with American writer John Williams's novel *Stoner*. Published in 1965, it had modest sales and disappeared without trace. Until 2013, when, in reprint, it suddenly became a runaway bestseller, billed as 'the greatest novel you've never heard of'. It's basically the Rodriguez story of publishing, except that unlike the reclusive American folk singer, Williams was already dead when his moment of recognition came.

Stoner is one of about a billion novels I've never read, and may never get to. In China, mega-rich tycoons are apparently overcoming this problem by appointing 'reading staff' of up to three people. Their job is to read and summarise the latest releases for their boss, who can then go on to casually introduce these books in conversation at dinner parties and give the impression of astonishing erudition, though perhaps not necessarily someone you'd want to be stuck next to the whole evening.

On the one hand, there's obviously something rather depressing about that situation. On the other hand, though, isn't it wonderful that books still carry so much social cachet that you'd want to pay someone so that you can pretend to have read them? I'd quite like a job as a member of a reading staff, though I bet they'd make you start with *A Brief History of Time*.

8

The End of the World

A couple of years ago I interviewed a South African Doomsday Prepper. Doomsday Preppers are people who believe the entire social and economic system is going to collapse at some point in the near future. They will be the only people to survive because they have stockpiled weaponry and canned food and built underground bunkers and, presumably, taught their kids how to entertain themselves without PlayStations.

Doomsday Preppers are extremely vague about what will cause the breakdown of society, though on Prepper websites they gesture meaningfully at everything from earthquakes to the collapse of Lehman Brothers to the ascendancy of Miley Cyrus. Some of them refer to the society-ending event as TEOTWAWKI, a catchy little acronym short for The End Of The World As We Know It, pronounced Tee-Ought-Walk-Ee.

Having spent a bit of time in this online community, I can confidently assure you that you are *toast* when TEOTWAWKI hits. Oh, you have a few cans of tuna? Big whoop. Do you know how to use instant mashed pota-toes to stem a gushing wound? Could you fashion a rudimentary fridge from clay pots? I thought not.

The Prepper I interviewed was called Giles, and he seemed quite nor-mal. I never met him face to face, but I did not picture him having a beard down to his knees and cradling a sawn-off shotgun while peering through his letterbox with haunted eyes. He just seemed sort of *organised*, like someone who might do rather well in a corporate team-building exercise. He told me he was focusing on cultivating 'a source of potable water and means to obtaining fresh food', because 'when the system breaks it will not help to go to Checkers for your food'.

Giles made it sound like TEOTWAWKI would happen extremely sud-denly, as if one minute you'd be browsing for kale in the Checkers veggie aisle and the next minute you'd be bartering sex for a handful of beans in an abandoned quarry.

He seemed to be a bit torn about whether he should warn others to make similar preparations, or not warn them so that there would be more beans to go around after TEOTWAWKI. 'I wish they would listen,' he told me, not altogether convincingly. 'But there are too many people. The only way that a few people can survive is if our numbers are greatly reduced.'

Giles wouldn't tell me his full name. Maybe he thought it would be weird if his co-workers knew that the quiet dude in IT was spending his weekends learning how to home-deliver babies in a post-apocalyptic world. I could understand that. What I found harder to understand is why he was *bothering*.

If I was reasonably convinced that society was about to collapse, as Giles was, I might well decide to devote my life to consequence-free hedonism. Sex, drugs, rock 'n' roll, and not a sniff of a retirement annuity. Why not? I put it to Giles that maybe he should abandon his preparations and throw himself into the Amy Winehouse lifestyle plan. He was unmoved. 'If any-thing it has caused me to act less recklessly,' he said. (By 'it' he meant 'living with the conviction that the world is about to end'.) 'I want myself and my children to survive. I feel I need to tackle this situation in a cool, calculated way. The future holds many perils.'

Those perils are precisely what make me *not* want to survive the collapse of society. Preppers make the post-TEOTWAWKI landscape sound like a remarkably unpleasant place to live. In their vision there are mobs of hunger-crazed looters roaming the ruined streets in feral packs, desperate to get a nibble on your ankle if they root you out of your smelly, dark, underground bunker. I've already been to Rocking the Daisies, thanks.

Having said that, I almost want our social and economic systems to implode just because I will feel so bad for Preppers if they *don't*. How much will it suck for them if everything just carries on ticking along merrily like normal? Try selling a house with a vast underground lair without everyone suspecting you have been using it to imprison a secret family for decades.

I interviewed Giles on the eve of December 21 2012, the date the Ancient Mayans had allegedly pinpointed as marking the end of the world. Historians protested in vain that the Ancient Mayans had said nothing of the kind. The idea stemmed from, among other sources, a date inscription on a Mayan archaeological site that was misinterpreted. The whole mix-up was a bit like when you get a Chinese tattoo that you think means 'Dance as if nobody's watching' and then years later you find out it actually reads 'Fuckpig'.

That didn't stop hundreds of people around the world from gathering on December 20 2012 at special sites believed to offer magical immunity against the apocalypse. When midnight hit and absolutely nothing happened, how did they feel? Was there a crushing sense of anticlimax or overwhelming relief? I think if I were standing atop a freezing mountain, clutching my snacks for an apocalypse that never came, what I would feel most of all would be: silly. It's just so *embarrassing*.

Due to my family history, I have significant empathy for people in the thrall of false prophecies. My mother was born and raised in a small village called Nås, in Sweden, which is notable for one reason only – a reason my siblings and I were blissfully unaware of when we resolved to visit it a few years ago.

We reached my mother's village on a freezing mid-winter's afternoon, with the light already beginning to fade. It was, in truth, less a 'village' than the setting for a Grimm's fairy tale in which children would end up eaten: a cluster of houses amidst deep forest. At the centre looms a Lutheran church. My grandparents are buried in its graveyard. Their single grave was quite hard to locate because the inhabitants of the village appeared to have been dying like flies over the past centuries and almost everyone had basically the same name.

My twin sister and I had chosen to wear light canvas pumps; as we plodded ankle-deep in Swedish snow down the rows of unidentifiable villager graves, a spirit of mutiny began to swell. Just as we were about to chuck it all in and go and eat herring somewhere warm, we found it: a single, humble grave.

Over the course of 30 years, lichen had overgrown our grandparents' names. We scratched at it ineffectually and then sort of stood around, wondering what people did in such situations. We hadn't thought to bring flowers. In the end I stuck a business card among some weeds. I couldn't imagine the groundskeeper coming upon it and being moved to tears, but it seemed better than nothing.

My mother and her parents didn't even live in the village itself. They lived almost 5 kilometres outside, deeper still into the forest, like goblins. In deepening darkness we set out to find it, armed only with a set of topological markers breezily delivered by my mother, who hadn't set foot there for 30 years: 'A large lake will appear on your left. A small hill follows. Ahead, a stretch of open fields.' It was like being directed on a quest by King Arthur. More incredibly, the directions proved unerringly accurate.

Having disappointingly discovered that the family home was not made of gingerbread, we returned to the village to wait for a train that would

47

allegedly take us to a neighbouring village, which offered some form of hostelry to weary travellers. I say 'allegedly' because as we waited in pitch darkness and thickly falling snow on an abandoned platform, it began to seem utterly inconceivable that such a train existed.

Perhaps this was an elaborate practical joke on the part of my mother. People who found it necessary to travel between these outposts probably did so on skis – or centaurs. We would die here, on this platform, in our inadequate winter clothing, and our remains would be scooped into the same grave as our grandparents, memorialised only by an unlaminated business card.

The train came, of course, dead on time. These are the people who gave us the Volvo, after all. With no warning it roared out of the snowy darkness, a sleek modern machine ferrying us in warmth and comfort from Nås to the next village. On the other side, the proprietor of our guest house was waiting to pick us up. A middle-aged woman who spoke impeccable English, she had one burning and understandable question: 'Why on earth did you go to Nås?'

We explained the family history. 'Ah, I see,' she said. And then added, with an air of significance: 'It is a strange place, Nås.'

It wasn't like we disagreed, but her tone suggested she meant something ... *more*.

'Why do you say that?' I asked.

She twisted to look at me. 'Your mother didn't tell you?'

Those are words that rarely bode well. It seemed distinctly unlikely that she would go on to cry: 'Why, Nås boasts the highest concentration of Nobel Prize-winners in the Western Hemisphere!' or something similarly upbeat. And indeed she did not.

What she told us was that my mother comes from the most gullible village in Sweden. She didn't put it quite like that, but it wasn't hard to read between the lines. In 1896 the villagers of Nås were visited by a guy called Olaf Henrik Larsson, who told them that if they packed up and moved to the Holy Land, it would hasten the Second Coming of Christ.

'See you there!' responded many, promptly selling all their worldly possessions and trekking off to Jerusalem.

I don't doubt their religious fervour, but having been to Nås, part of me wonders if they were also secretly motivated by the prospect of better weather. Sadly for them, Jerusalem turned out not to be the land of milk and honey they expected. A few years into their stay a devastating plague of locusts stripped the area of all vegetation. *An actual plague of locusts.* I mean, talk about an omen. When you come expecting Jesus, and what you get are locusts, someone is sending you a pretty definite message.

Jesus never showed up. Some of the villagers trudged back to Nås in humiliation. Others died out there, in a strange religious colony in Jerusalem, thousands of miles from the village where they were born.

'We didn't really talk about it,' my mother responded gruffly when I phoned her that night from our guest house. She was at home in Simonstown, in Cape Town. I could picture her sitting in the lounge with my father, our dog Jumble at her feet: she, another citizen of Nås who left the snowy forest for a strange, hot country.

'My mother always said it was a source of great shame to the village,' she said.

My mother is the staunchest atheist I know: a woman with a steely, sharp mind who has no patience for superstition, for nonsense, for wishy-washy thinking. As I put down the phone that night, I thought I understood a bit more about why she was the way she was.

The people of Nås were neither the first nor the last to be sold a dream. *Destroy your crops and kill your cattle,* the prophet Nongqawuse told the Xhosa people only a few decades before the Nås villagers made their pilgrimage. *In return, the spirits will sweep the British settlers into the sea, your crops will grow back tenfold, and your kraals will overflow with fat cows.* The resulting famine killed more than two-thirds of the population of British Kaffraria. And those British settlers went nowhere.

We modern folk may look back and scoff at such ignorance from our place of light and reason and Wikipedia. But are we any less susceptible to such dreams?

Buy this face cream, advertisers tell us. *You won't be old any more.*

Invest in my Ponzi scheme and you'll have your own castle by Christmas.

One spritz of this cheap deodorant and women will experience an uncontrollable urge to mate with you.

Vote for our party or a terrible darkness will befall the land and you'll have to move to Australia.

It's all the same old shit, except at least Nongqawuse and Olaf Henrik Larsson actually believed in what they were trying to get folk to sign up to.

I may think that Doomsday Preppers like Giles need their heads checked. But then I remember that in my veins runs the blood of a Swedish village that moved to Jerusalem to meet Christ, and in my hands rests a credit card that just shelled out hundreds of rand for a skin treatment to freeze time.

9

Goldilocks and the Endless Unanswered Questions

The thing about fairy tales is that their whole purpose is to impart some clear moral instruction to kids, but looking back from adulthood I still don't have a clue what some of them mean.

I find Goldilocks and the Three Bears particularly confusing. In the way it is usually told, Goldilocks, a flaxen-tressed little girl, wanders into the forest by herself. In some versions she gets lost and in others she is simply a busybody. Either way, she comes across a cottage of some description. The door is unlocked, so Goldilocks enters.

Three bears live in the place: a small one, a medium-sized one and a big one. In the original story, credited to British author Robert Southey in 1837, the three bears were all male. They were 'bachelors' who lived together, and I think we all know what that means.

In later renditions, crushed by heteronormativity, they became a sweet little bear family: Mama, Papa and Baby Bear. They are partial to a steaming bowl of porridge for breakfast. On this particular day, however, they make porridge for their breakfast and then *go for a walk*. While it seems churlish to pick holes in a plot centred on talking bears who live like humans, this is one of the most implausible parts of the narrative.

The explanation offered is that they go for a walk because the porridge is too hot to eat and needs to cool down. Frankly, this raises more questions than it answers. What kind of nuclear porridge requires the interval of a forest hike to lower its temperature? Who cooks hot food and promptly goes for a walk, other than perhaps someone with a strange eating disorder? Why didn't they just blow on it impatiently for a bit, like the rest of us?

By the time they get back from the walk, there's no way that porridge won't be icy. Cold porridge is disgusting, like eating clumps of grey snot. Some people, I acknowledge, actually like cold oat products. But then the whole point is that you don't cook them at all. If the element of porridge that the Bears wanted to dispense with was its comforting warmth, Mama Bear could simply have poured some rolled oats into a bowl and sloshed in some milk. She might have considered soaking the oats in apple juice beforehand for a cosmopolitan twist.

It is usually Mama Bear who is credited with making the porridge, which suggests an adherence to traditional gender roles in the Bear household. I'd like to know whose idea the walk was, though. I can imagine Mama Bear throwing up her paws in frustration.

'You *always* do this!' she hisses at Papa Bear. 'I spend half an hour slaving over the stove to make your porridge, and then all of a sudden you decide it's the ideal moment to take a *fucking walk*!'

'Not in front of Baby Bear, please,' Papa sighs, wearily rubbing his face. 'You're the one always bitching that we don't spend enough time together as a family! Then I suggest we take *one walk* together and suddenly that's a problem too! Honestly, Marlene, sometimes I don't even know what you want from me any more!'

'Get your shoes, Baby Bear,' Mama snaps grimly. 'Your *father* has decided this is the *ideal opportunity* for a *family walk*, so of course that's what we're going to do.'

And off they march, weighed down with resentment but determined to make the best of it.

Enter Goldilocks. She cases the joint, sees the coast is clear, and slips inside.

There, she beholds a wonderful treat lying on the table: three bowls of porridge, already dished up.

'Get inside my belly!' she cries, or words to that effect, and prepares to smash Papa Bear's porridge into her face. But after her first spoon, she realises this isn't going to work. The porridge is too hot. This suggests that the time between the Bears' exit and the entrance of Goldilocks must have been a matter of mere minutes, if that. The girl was playing with fire.

It is understandable that Papa Bear's porridge would be too hot to eat, given this timeline of events. What happens next, however, is beyond comprehension. Goldilocks digs into Mama Bear's porridge – and finds that it is *too cold*.

How is it possible that two bowls of porridge dished within seconds of each other could have reached such vastly different resting temperatures minutes later? One is scorching; one is freezing.

This bizarre temperature discrepancy does not end there. Pushing away Mama Bear's icy bowl with revulsion – further proof that cold porridge is generally considered deeply unappealing – Goldilocks makes the happy yet inexplicable discovery that Baby Bear's porridge is *just right*. Not too hot, not too cold.

What's going on here, physicists? This is horseshit, pure and simple.

But we press on. Goldilocks has greedily slurped down every last morsel of Baby Bear's porridge, and now her eyes fall upon the Bears' lounge suite. That the sight of three chairs – *chairs*, for God's sake – could evoke such excitement within her suggests strongly to me that Goldilocks is from a poignantly underprivileged background. She sees three chairs, and her response is: 'Score! I'll have me a go on one of those!'

Though this furniture-induced elation prompts sympathy, her subsequent actions do not. Big Bear's chair, which I picture as something like the Iron Throne from *Game of Thrones*, is furiously rejected for being too hard. Mama Bear's chair is too soft, presumably because Mama Bear likes to slump prostrate after a hard day of cooking hot meals that go ignored. Baby Bear's chair is just right, so Goldilocks settles in for a pretty intense sit.

She breaks the chair. There is no indication that Goldilocks is a girl of unusual weight. If anything, her habit of scavenging for strangers' breakfasts suggests the opposite. The chair can't have been too small because we've already been assured that it was 'just right', and otherwise she could have been having a relaxing moment on Mama's La-Z-Boy. She must have been riding that chair like a wild horse. It breaks.

Goldilocks decides to upgrade her sit to a lie-down. *Magie vol, ogies toe* – we've all been there. There's nothing quite as nice as a post-breakfast nap on a weekend. She climbs the stairs and hits the jackpot: the Bears' bedroom. Here the Bears apparently sleep in three separate beds in a row, which speaks volumes about the state of Mama and Papa's relationship.

The first bed precious Goldilocks tries is dismissed for being 'too high'. This is an odd bed-related complaint, but perhaps we can make sense of it if we assume that Goldilocks is too short to clamber onto Papa Bear's bed with ease. Mama Bear's bed earns her displeasure, however, by being too low, which suggests that it may be some sort of futon. Perhaps Mama Bear's chiropractor has advised her to seek out a more structured mattress to ease the spinal damage caused by perpetual slumping in her flabby armchair.

But Baby Bear's bed is perfectly to her tastes, and Goldilocks – apparently untroubled by the prospect of imminent discovery, or too stupid to have contemplated this course of events – falls into a dreamy slumber.

Enter the Bears.

Having finally completed their forest perambulation, the Bears are back, slavering in anticipation of their frosty porridge. No sooner do they enter the house, however, than they sense that something is terribly wrong. As an amateurish criminal, Goldilocks has made several elementary mistakes. For one, she has left the porridge bowls in quite a state, such that her little porridge-tasting programme is instantly apparent.

Each Bear's attention is rather selfishly only on their personal bowl, rather than appraising the scene as a whole.

'Who's been eating my porridge?' growls Papa Bear.

Mama Bear doesn't give a shit about Papa's porridge problems. 'Who's been eating *my* porridge?' she wails. At the back of her mind there is probably also a dawning sense of vindication, since everything is already pointing to a strong argument for hot food being consumed within a reasonable period of its creation.

That, and they definitely need to start looking into a Trellidor, because this woodland community is clearly not what it used to be.

Baby Bear is the real victim here, however. 'Who's been eating my porridge and eaten it all up?' he howls. Baby Bear is mad for porridge, it emerges. There is no time to console the ursine youngster, however, because CSI: Bear has already kicked into gear.

Papa Bear is able to perceive *at a single glance* that his chair has been sat in. Mama Bear apparently boasts the same facility when it comes to forensic investigation. Again, Baby Bear's level of personal injury is far more severe than his parents' – his chair is literally in pieces on the floor – but the older Bears' singular focus is on how they have been wronged by a stranger's buttocks pressing into their armchairs.

Charging up the stairs into the bedroom, the crime-fighting trio find their target. Goldilocks is still snoring away in Baby Bear's bed, implausibly undisturbed by their previous shouts of anger. This girl could kip for the first team.

There, the Bears unleash thunderous roars of rage, which finally have the result of rousing our narcoleptic heroine. One can imagine that being woken by three bears hurling abuse at you would be both unexpected and unpleasant. Then again, as discussed, Goldilocks has revealed herself to be an utterly inept and reckless home intruder, and it's hard to summon much pity. As ye sow, so shall ye reap, to quote another popular fairy tale.

And what Goldilocks is reaping is a massive can of Bear whup-ass. Except that that's not at all what happens. The Bears, despite collectively outstripping Goldilocks by a considerable margin in both brawn and brains, apparently stand by helplessly while the fiendish little blonde zips out of the bedroom, down the stairs and exits the front door. Neither is there any indication that they give chase.

Goldilocks gets away scot-free. Oh, sure, she's all *traumatised* and shit, but there is no penalty for the string of criminal offences she has racked up: breaking and entering, theft, illegal squatting. She is not hauled off to any woodland juvenile detention centre. The Bears do not press charges.

What exactly is the moral of the story here? Is it that you shouldn't enter people's houses, eat their food and destroy their furniture? For one thing, that's hardly a quotidian scenario for most kids. For another, the fact that Goldilocks is not ripped limb from limb by the avenging Bears really muddles the message. Don't do that bad thing – but if you do, absolutely nothing will happen to you. Quite frankly, it breeds a culture of irresponsibility.

The other weird thing is that the enduring legacy of Goldilocks in the English language places the focus on a completely different aspect of the story. A 'Goldilocks planet' is one where the astral positioning is *just right*: not too far from a star, and not too close. A 'Goldilocks economy' is moderate and centrist: *just right*. These are, objectively, good things.

This is mad. A Goldilocks planet should refer to a terrestrial sphere where the rule of law has completely broken down. A Goldilocks economy should be one on the brink of collapse from looting and pillaging.

But instead our language tacitly celebrates Goldilocks' pickiness on her crime spree. I'm having none of it. If I ever have the opportunity to tell that story to a child, I'll be making a number of significant changes. Starting with that porridge bullshit.

10

Past Imperfect, Present Tense

Few people would disagree that life in the future has proved disappointing in many respects. Yes, yes, more people have *human rights* and stuff, but will a human right fly you to your holiday house in space?

I am, of course, alive to the ways in which the present is better than the past. Anyone who needs convincing on this score should read Steven Pinker's *The Better Angels of our Nature*, in which he compellingly sets out the case that we are living in the least violent period of human history.

The best bits of Pinker's book are where he reminds us how awful things were in the Middle Ages, when everyone was basically just revolting. You may not be aware, for instance, that the phrase 'to cut off one's nose to spite one's face' actually originates from *a real thing* – though it wasn't auto-inflicted, as the phrasing suggests. In the Middle Ages, cutting off someone else's nose was a perfectly unremarkable act of revenge. Pinker notes, in fact, that so many people had their noses lopped off that whole books and medical conferences were devoted to plotting ways to grow back noses.

Nowadays some cunning wizard would just make you a new one. An engineer could probably 3D-print you one to your specification while you leafed through the latest *Hello*. You can have a whole face transplant, for heaven's sake, though we know that doesn't always work out as well as you'd think. A fascinating July 2014 *GQ* feature on one of the first people to receive a full face transplant, Richard Norris, painted a sad and strange picture of his new life.

Norris's old face, the result of shooting himself at point-blank range, was almost indescribable: like something Salvador Dali would place in the middle of a desert landscape. The new face is quite dreamy, akin to that of a male soap star who has had some cosmetic surgery.

Considering Norris claimed to have spent the last 15 years living as a hermit in a full-face mask, you'd think he'd have been living it up now. The problem was that he was expected to take awfully good care of his new face, partly because he was a walking advert for the technology and partly because the procedure left him incredibly sensitive to infection. He wasn't supposed to tan, or smoke, or drink, or do anything fun with his face other than keep it screwed to his skull for people to gawk at.

Except that he did smoke. And when he suggested the *GQ* journalist take a drive with him, away from his overbearing mother, Norris insisted on stopping at a liquor store to stock up on whisky. He said it was to relieve the dryness in his throat, and then proceeded to pour it straight into his stomach via a special feeding tube. Then he passed out.

The feeling you were left with was that Norris's life with a new face wasn't all that great. But maybe this is the problem with progress and evolution and all that jazz: there's no getting away from human nature. You can slap a new face on us, but we're still the same old anxious, strange creatures we've always been.

But at least the option of a new nose is available to us now, and at least it's more common for us to wreak vengeance on others through cutting Facebook posts rather than cutting off bits of their face.

I was persuaded of the merits of modern life on a daily basis when I had a research job that required me to read newspaper clippings from the 18th century. Let me repeat: life in the olden days was *totally shit*. Everyone was racist and sexist and kept dying in horse-related incidents.

But that doesn't mean that the present has lived up to my expectations of the future in the slightest. I can scarcely believe that more than 100 years since Henry Ford popped his first automobile off the assembly line, we are still relying on *cars* to get around.

Admittedly, some of my disappointment in this regard may be attributable to the fact that I am an absolutely abominable driver. As a militant feminazi it's frustrating to so completely fit one of the most boring, offensive stereotypes about women, but there you have it. I can't even fight it. I listen to sexist jokes about women being unable to parallel park and all I can do is mutter 'fair point' through gritted teeth.

For me the most exciting development in automobile evolution since car radios has been the emergence of the self-driving car. I wish Google would get busy mass-producing those bad boys instead of hogging them to itself. The first incarnation of self-driving cars let humans take control if they needed to all of a sudden, but the latest ones don't even have a steering wheel or brakes.

I can imagine that the experience of being chauffeured around in a self-driving car must be disconcerting, to say the least. Unless you're as awful a driver as I am, they're going to be a hard sell because they require humanoids to do exactly what we've feared most since the dawn of science fiction: place ourselves entirely in the hands of a really clever robot.

This is daunting not just because we all know how often technology gets glitchy but because we all know how the story ends. The robots rise up and kill us when we prove unworthy of their service.

Google claims that only two of its driverless cars have ever been in accidents, and both times it was the fault of other humans. But the company would say that, wouldn't it? If driverless cars do get into scrapes that are their own fault, though, who takes the liability? You, sitting blamelessly with your hands folded in your lap, or the robot? This is actually a question that is being pondered at this very moment by lawyers and robotics experts. So far the consensus seems to be that self-driving cars would have to become separate insurable entities.

Or, to put it in a far more chilling way, we would have to grant legal personhood to robots. And the no-no feeling this idea induces would be precisely what robots rights activists would point to while they crush us to death with their robot claws when the robot uprising comes.

But for now, the problem seems to be this: if self-driving cars are ever to take off, we need absolutely everyone to have them. Human-controlled cars would have to be wiped off the roads overnight. Otherwise you just *know* your sleek self-driven steed would be rear-ended by some douche with a personalised number plate in about five minutes.

There's no sign that self-driving cars are becoming the vehicular status quo any time soon, which leaves us back where we started, with our boring old transport systems. In some ways I feel like we might even be going backwards, at least aesthetically. If you looked at a picture from the 1930s and saw a mighty Zeppelin moored to the spire of the Empire State Building – as indeed happened a few times – wouldn't that fit your mental picture of The Future a lot better than, say, the 5pm traffic jam on the N2?

I am old enough to remember the excitement when the Segway was first released in 2001. For those of you who might not recall, the Segway is a two-wheeled, self-balancing, battery-powered electric vehicle invented by American entrepreneur Dean Kamen, and now almost exclusively ridden by security guards in underground car parks.

I vividly recall the suspense before its unveiling. After all, this was the follow-up invention from the man who brought us a wheelchair that could climb stairs. A freakin' wheelchair that could climb chairs! Who knew what he'd think of next?

The day when the Segway was unleashed upon the public was one of the most thrilling of my life. 'This will change everything!' I babbled to anyone who would listen. 'Bring on the complete overhaul of urban transport systems!' What we were on the threshold of, I believed, was nothing less than a mobile revolution.

In this assessment I was, of course, not alone. Urban planners were talking about designing *cities* around Segways. Until they saw one. Kamen himself predicted that the Segway 'will be to the car what the car was to the horse and buggy'. Which, in the light of the Segway's spectacular failure, is a bit like me saying 'this book will be to literature what literature was to scratching in the dirt with twigs'.

We must face facts. The Segway has bombed on an epic scale. They thought they would sell 100 000 of them in the first year and they managed to unload 30 000 in the first six years. I'm no mathematician, but that's, like, three a year.

The reasons for this monumental fuck up are, with the unflinching clarity of hindsight, not terribly hard to see. The fundamental issue is that nobody, and I do mean nobody, is ever going to look sexy gently perambulating down the road on a Segway. James Dean would look dorky on a Segway.

Then there was that sad and embarrassing incident in 2010 when Jimi Heselden, who ended up buying the Segway company, fell off a cliff while riding a Segway and died. (I was inexplicably reminded of this episode in mid-2014 when the author of *How to Survive the Bulls of Pamplona* was gored by a bull in Pamplona.)

I remain sad that Segways haven't taken off, though I recognise the adverse impact on our economy if everyone was trundling across the country at a top speed of 20 kilometres per hour. I'd like to think we'd be a different kind of society, though. Gentler. More peaceful. You can't imagine someone on a Segway whipping out a hockey stick to beat a fellow Seg-wayer to death at a traffic light, can you?

Then again, they used to sell that exact shtick about bus travel – confoundingly, since anyone who has ever been on a long-haul bus trip can tell you exactly what level of physical pain and emotional anguish is involved. Greyhound Canada launched an extensive advertising campaign in 2008 with the slogan 'There's a reason you've never heard of bus rage', intended to positively contrast the soothing pleasures of bus travel with the stresses of highway driving.

No sooner had they unveiled this winning campaign than a passenger on a Greyhound bus was unexpectedly beheaded by the man sitting next to him. Vince Li then proceeded to wave the decapitated head at other passengers. When police eventually detained him, he was eating bits of his victim's face from a plastic bag.

When you think about Vince Li snacking on facial features as if they were biltong snapstix, you lose a bit of smugness about how far we've come from the Middle Ages. After all, there's no suggestion that people *ate* each other's noses after they'd hacked them off back then. They probably just left them lying there on the horse path, marinating in someone's urine.

This is why we humans can't have nice things. Stick us in a self-driving car all you want, but maybe we're doomed to be the same old face-carvers we've always been.

11

More Bang from Your Buck

I've got a poor head for figures. It is only thanks to South Africa's Deputy President Cyril Ramaphosa that I was recently made aware of the value of wildlife – in economic terms, I mean. In April 2012, it was reported that Ramaphosa had bid R19,5 million at an auction for a buffalo and her calf.

The response from large swathes of the South African public was one of outrage that Ramaphosa would be shelling out these kinds of bucks for something as apparently trivial as a buffalo while loads of other people were poor. He wasn't deputy president at the time, though one of the reasons why people found his wealth display unpalatable was due to the incongruity of the fact that he used to be an earnest trade unionist sounding off about the evils of capital.

It all got decidedly stickier a few months later, when striking miners at Lonmin – the platinum producer that Ramaphosa sat on the board of – were shot dead by police while asking for an increase in their paltry wages.

Against that backdrop, Ramaphosa's buffalo shopping understandably took on a darker hue, and it's no coincidence he apologised for the buffalo-bidding episode a month after the Marikana massacre but five months after the actual incident.

Still, few people seemed to show a commensurate interest in what the white Lonmin executives were doing with their ill-gotten shekels at the time. Nobody bitched about the man who actually ended up buying the buffalo, Jaco Troskie, who forked out no less than 200 buffaloes for the buffalo, which is to say R20 million. Troskie is the son of Boet Troskie, best known for having produced two *The Gods Must Be Crazy* films.

You know the flicks I mean. The first one starts with a 'Bushman' getting clocked on the noggin by a Coke bottle falling from the sky. It's an unsubtle metaphor for the encroachment of modernity on a wildly romanticised 'traditional' way of life. Or as the film's poster put it: 'The critics are raving ... The natives are restless ... *and the laughter is non-stop!*' The initial film grossed $100 million worldwide when it came out in 1980. This makes it the most commercially successful film in the history of South African filmmaking and possibly also among the most commercially successful films in the history of the world to be made of 109 minutes of patronising racial stereotypes.

At the end of the film, the 'Bushman' is offered a heap of money from kindly whites he has assisted during the course of his magical quest to dispose of the Coke bottle. He rejects the cash. 'Bushmen don't know about money,' his translator explains. 'Bushmen don't need these things.'

Virtually the same interaction, conveniently enough, appears to have played out between the real-life San actor – N!Xau – and the film's makers, since N!xau reportedly received less than $2 000 out of that $100 million for his role, though this was apparently later supplemented somewhat.

(N!Xau became wildly popular, incidentally, with Asian audiences. He went on to make a 1994 film with a Hong Kong production company called *The Gods Must Be Funny in China*, in which he becomes an expert in martial arts. I would shell out a few buffaloes of my own to see that movie.)

Anyway, the point is that it's not like Jaco Troskie's vaults of money are exactly untainted by exploitative baggage either, but I didn't hear any carping when Jaco rode his hugundously expensive buffalo out of the auction.

What shocked me most about Buffalogate, to be honest, was how expensive buffaloes were. The buffalo in question was apparently the biggest in Africa, but I'd need it to be made out of platinum with a caramel centre to convince me that was a reasonable price. Even the dude who sold it seemed taken aback, since he was reported as *bursting into tears of joy* when the auctioneer's gavel fell. I'd also cry with happiness if I unloaded a glorified cow for 20 million.

Ramaphosa seemed to suggest afterwards that he'd just allowed himself to get a bit carried away. 'Like any businessman, you must know when to stop,' he said. And who among us *hasn't* been tempted to stick their hands up when the bidding reaches R19,5 million for a gregarious bovid?

Troskie's buffalo wasn't even the most expensive buffalo sold in South Africa in recent years. About 18 months later, billionaire Johann Rupert spent R40 million on a buffalo bull. This capital outlay for something you cannot live in, fly on or teach to present its hoof on demand!

Obviously, buffalo are quite rare. You don't bump into them on the way to Spar. They're not *that* rare, though. On conservation lists they're classed as a species of 'Least Concern', which comes across as quite an unfeeling phrase, so be sure not to tell your buffalo.

Apparently buffalo are a simply spectacular investment, however. The average return on buffalo wildly out-performs property. It's the same for all rare game. In fact, research undertaken by Moneyweb in 2013 specified that the annual return on black impala was 130%. Property has a typical return of 10%.

Why are we not told this?

Obviously richies know all about it, since they seem to be snapping up antelope the way you and I buy milk. I feel like we humble members of the proletariat, however, are being given exceptionally poor investment advice.

'A two-bedroom lock-up-and-go in Woodstock?' financial managers should say sceptically. 'You *could*, of course. But you'd be mad not to go with this breeding pair of swart rooibok instead.'

There would, obviously, be two major obstacles to the establishment of this kind of investment portfolio. The first is that you can't get a mortgage for swart rooibok, so you'd just have to have the capital on hand: yet *another* way that the rich get richer while the rest of us moulder in wildlife-deprived financial mediocrity.

The second is that my body corporate won't even let me and my girlfriend get a Jack Russell, and I'm not convinced we'd be able to smuggle an antelope up the back stairs undetected.

Until the rest of us get in on this racket, the Ramaphosas and Ruperts will undoubtedly keep filling their bottomless money-wells with bucks from bucks. Occupy buffalo auctions, I say.

12

Don'ts for Wives

I once had a work colleague named Sara who was from Eritrea and spoke a very limited and idiosyncratic species of English. We were ushers in a London cinema, fortunately, so she wasn't required to deliver Shakespearian aphorisms on a daily basis. Between shifts, or when things were slow, we'd both whip out books and have a sneaky read. For months and months Sara painstakingly worked her way through a tiny, hard-covered volume. It was the kind of thing you'd find in the novelty gift section of a bookstore, and it was titled *Don'ts for Wives*, the replica of a book published in 1913.

The original book was entirely serious, but in its reprinted incarnation it's the kind of wry satirical present that modern young women give each other. To modern young women the advice it offers is belly-clutchingly absurd.

Don't vegetate as you grow older if you live in the country, author Blanche Ebutt counsels. *Some women are like cows, but there is really no need to stagnate.*

If you *are* like a cow, though, which Blanche seems to grudgingly acknowledge as a possibility, why shouldn't you vegetate? Take a load off, cow-woman. Ruminate. Masticate. Fill your four stomachs with soft country grass.

Don't persist in having mushrooms on the table when you know they always make your husband ill, runs another sensible tip. *They may be **your** favourite dish, but is it worth it?*

Well, obviously if your husband has some kind of violent mushroom allergy, you'd have to be borderline psychotic to keep dishing up porcini pasta seven days a week. Unless you were trying to kill him, which is not a scenario that Blanche entertains.

She does, however, seem to anticipate that life as a mushroom-starved wife may not bring you the blissful fulfilment you crave.

Don't spend half the morning in bed because there is 'nothing to get up for', Blanche warns, which sounds like a textbook diagnosis of clinical depression to me. Not that Blanche has any sympathy. Get up, cow-woman, and take up your position with your ear pressed to the door to await your husband's return from work. *Don't let him search the house for you*, Blanche advises. (Just how massive was Blanche's pad? It would take roughly three seconds for anyone to find me in my flat.) *Listen for his latch-key and meet him on the threshold.*

You get the picture.

It was a source of some concern to me, however, that Sara did not appear to be reading *Don'ts For Wives* in the throes of riotous amusement. Indeed, I never saw the faintest smile cross her lips. She read the book in a posture of deep concentration, and – far more troubling – occasionally pencilled notes as she went.

It began to dawn on me, with great alarm, that perhaps Sara was not approaching *Don'ts for Wives* in the appropriate spirit of hilarity. I couldn't be sure, though, because in other respects Sara appeared to be a modern young woman. In one other respect, to be precise.

One day, when we were casually counting ticket stubs, she turned to me and my friend Cristina and inquired if it was normal for one's body to shake uncontrollably at the point of orgasm.

She didn't phrase it quite like that. In rudimentary English the question sounded so filthy that I'd blush to type it here. Blanche wouldn't approve.

That line of inquiry led me to believe that Sara was a woman of the world. But the dedicated study she gave to *Don'ts for Wives* made me suspect otherwise. In fairness, there was absolutely nothing to indicate that *Don'ts for Wives* shouldn't be treated as an earnest how-to guide. There wasn't a comical illustration on the front of a man projectile-vomiting mushrooms. There wasn't a jacket sticker bellowing BUY THIS FOR A LARF! All things considered, I saw no reason why Sara – as a foreigner to the UK and someone with only a passing acquaintance with the English language – should be expected to be in on the joke.

The notion weighed heavily on me. I thought about bringing it up but I had no idea how to phrase it.

'Hey Sara,' I might begin, while we were cashing up. 'You know that book you've been reading for the last ten weeks, *Don'ts for Wives*?'

'Yes?' she'd say, looking up from her piles of coins.

'It reflects a version of marriage from almost 100 years ago,' I'd say. 'The thing is, it doesn't have to be like that any more.'

This imagined conversation made me cringe. Wasn't it terribly arrogant of me to assume that Sara needed me to emancipate her from her mental shackles? Maybe everything Sara read in *Don'ts for Wives* chimed perfectly with her vision of harmonious wedlock. Perhaps she totally agreed with Blanche that one shouldn't *bother your husband with a stream of senseless chatter if you can see that he is very fatigued.*

After all, isn't one of the criticisms levelled against us Westernised feminists that we always think we know what's best for *all* women? Ripping off women's headscarves willy-nilly. Telling contented housewives that they should find some dregs of self-respect and train to be fighter pilots. Tearing copies of *Cosmo* out of the hands of teenage girls just looking for some decent hand-job tips and force-feeding them *The Female Eunuch* instead.

If Sara wanted to be a wife from 1913, then perhaps I should wish her all the best. Though she'd need to find an uncommonly rich husband to do Blanche proud, since she was learning lessons like *Don't let your servants use paraffin for fire-lighting purposes.*

It did grate me, though, that Sara appeared to be mentally training to be some man's docile slave. Someone who would perpetually put her husband's needs above her own; who would shape her entire life in his image; who would wait on him hand and foot and do everything possible to keep him fluffed in a perpetually jolly mood.

I started to consider the possibility that I was *jealous.* Not of Sara's future husband in particular, because I often found Sara a bit annoying, but of *all* husbands who managed to bag themselves this kind of wife.

My ex-girlfriend, an academic, often used to come home fulminating about the unfair advantage bestowed on her male colleagues with stay-at-home wives. I could totally see what she meant. There are still many men who have wives who essentially take care of absolutely everything in a man's life outside of his work. With all the boring behind-the-scenes shit taken care of, imagine how that must free you up for awesome stuff, like running multinational corporations?

Of course, this is also how rich people, regardless of marital status, operate. (I once read that actor Mark Wahlberg employs an assistant whose sole task is to wake him up on time in the morning.) But if you're not rich, the second-best thing must be to have a wife to serve you selflessly. There's an annoying saying that recognises how invaluable this labour can be to male success: 'Behind every great man, there's a woman.'

It also works the other way round. A *New York Times* article from December 2013 noted that some of the most successful women in American finance now have stay-at-home husbands. The article specified a 'direct link between their ability to achieve and their husbands' willingness to handle domestic duties'.

But it's a much, much rarer scenario, and the men interviewed for the article admitted feeling the social stigma of their roles. As a dude, you're still much more likely to end up with a stay-at-home wife than you are as a woman to meet a man who craves nothing more than to sit at home darning your socks.

It simply seems a bit unjust. The *Times* article recounted how one female banker told colleagues how she became irritated with her husband, who worked part-time, and told him: 'I wish I had a wife.'

I get it. Of course, as a gay woman, I am in the unique position of being *allowed* a wife, in South Africa at least. But it's my experience that many same-sex couples have a pesky habit of dividing domestic labour relatively equally. (My girlfriend would probably roll her eyes at this suggestion, since she cooks almost every scrap of food consumed in our household.)

It is, unfortunately, not part of the mainstream lesbian narrative that you will one day settle down with a woman well-versed in the *Don'ts for Wives*.

If push came to shove, of course, I'd way rather have a partner with a fulfilling career and a ton of interesting things to talk about in the evening when we're splitting the endless list of domestic chores that nobody had time to attend to during the day. I know many men feel the same way.

But it still irked me that Sara was dutifully educating herself in household servitude for a future husband, and I was pretty sure there wasn't a man out there doing the same for her.

As it turned out, though, my philosophical struggles came to nothing.

One evening, Sara closed her copy of *Don'ts for Wives* with a deep sigh, and turned to me.

'Rebecca,' she said, pointing to a word on the cover, 'what it means, "wives"?'

13

In Praise of Museums

I love a good museum. I have approached them with caution, though, ever since a man visiting the Fitzwilliam Museum in Cambridge in 2006 tripped over his shoelace, fell down the stairs and smashed three free-standing Qing vases. Dating back to the 17th century, they were worth a reported £100 000. It is such a nightmarish scenario that I try not to think about it very often.

Apparently people break exhibits at museums more often than you'd think. They also steal stuff. It's a major problem at the Vatican, where items are regularly posted back to them by regretful tourists with sticky fingers. I can imagine that nicking a holy relic from a site of spiritual pilgrimage must eat away at you slightly more than, say, shoplifting a Tempo from the 7-Eleven.

I wish that South Africa had more, and better, museums because some of the ones we have aren't great. Perhaps that's inevitable given our contested history. It took 42 years for the South African Museum in Cape Town to realise that its 'Bushman Diorama', presenting models of 'Bushmen' in their natural habitat as if they were stuffed animals, might be a tweetch offensive. When the diorama finally closed, in 2001, it was reported that it would be 'preserved untouched and archived'.

How creepy is that? Somewhere in the basement of the South African Museum, there apparently lurks this bizarre tableau, life-size figures trapped in a glass box for perpetuity. I'd hate to get locked in there overnight.

What should by rights be the most affecting museum in the country – Robben Island – is a shadow of what it could be. On recent occasions when I've been there, the group is whisked around at such breakneck speed that you barely have time to work up a meaningful tear in front of Nelson Mandela's cell because your ferry is about to leave.

At the risk of sounding like a buzzkill, I also find it in questionable taste that you can purchase Robben Island shot glasses from the on-site shop. While I've got no problems with the idea of toasting our democracy with a celebratory tequila, I can't imagine that there's a store at Auschwitz flogging branded beer mugs.

There are exceptions to this museum problem, of course. The Apartheid Museum in Johannesburg is powerful and moving and occasionally you stumble across smaller institutions that house unexpected gems. I'm a big fan of the National English Literary Museum in Grahamstown, where you can access the papers of many of South Africa's greatest writers: everything from their shopping lists to their personal letters.

It is infuriating, however, that the archives of some of the country's literary luminaries are sitting almost 15 000 kilometres away from South Africa. The Harry Ransom Center, at the University of Texas in Austin, has for years aggressively been seeking out and buying up the papers of distinguished African writers. Local institutions either lack the will or the financial muscle to compete. In 2011, 155 boxes of JM Coetzee's manuscripts, notebooks and letters were bought by the Ransom Center for $1,5 million. Ain't nobody got the money for a counter-offer in Coetzee's home country.

Why does this matter? Because it means that these exceedingly valuable resources will remain forever inaccessible to local scholars, unless they're fortunate enough to win a grant to travel to the US. I experienced this myself as a postgraduate student writing a thesis on South African short story master Herman Charles Bosman. Fancy a look at HCB's draft manuscripts and correspondence? By all means. You'll just have to fly to Texas.

It's doubly irritating because I cannot imagine that American scholars are beating down the Ransom Center's doors to pore over Bosman's papers. They're probably just gathering dust. Why do those imperialists always have to take our stuff?

Western museums are, of course, positively heaving with artefacts they looted from the developing world. The patronising argument to justify this has historically been that the holdings are in safer hands over there. Sometimes, unfortunately, this is true. It was heartbreaking to read of the 2013 torching by Mali rebels of Timbuktu libraries containing priceless ancient manuscripts, for instance.

But sometimes the West should just give that stuff back. One of my favourite museums in the world is the Pitt Rivers Museum in Oxford, in the UK. Its charm lies in the fact that it is basically a higgledy-piggledy repository of weird shit collected from around the world by an insane Victorian. By far the most amazing thing in it is its collection of shrunken heads from South America.

Amazonian tribesmen would cut off the heads of their fallen enemies, remove the brain, replace it with a wooden ball to keep the shape, and then boil the head to shrink it. (Nobody should tell the Islamic State about this, in case it gives them ideas.) There they hang in a glass case in the Pitt Rivers: tiny, decapitated, gruesome little heads shrouded in long dark hair. Those are the heads of *actual humans*. They are the body parts of dead people, who may well have existing relatives. It's a bit much, really. You can understand why a campaign has been brewing over the past decade to send them back to Ecuador and Peru.

The British Museum in London has an incredible collection of riches stolen from Africa. Their Benin bronzes are particularly awe-inspiring. One positive aspect of their plundering was that when they were brought to London in the 19th century, racist Brits were forced to face up to the uncomfortable reality of Africa's rich cultural history.

What the Benin bronzes suggest is that the average West African in 12 AD had a daily diary that looked something like: 'Wake up. Stretch limbs on hand-carved throne-bed. Eat feast. Create highly sophisticated terracotta full-face mask to wear in complex spiritual ceremony later. Engage in multi-layered abstract thought. Sculpt naturalistic representation of wood-god from burnished copper and polished jewels. Eat feast. Debate creation myths,' and so on.

Most of the rest of the world at this time was ticking off their two solitary quotidian to-do's of 'sit in own faeces' and 'root for grubs'.

Postcolonial Nigeria has understandably been a bit ticked off that the British Museum is hoarding its goodies. In an act of amazing cheek, the museum *sold back* 30 Benin bronzes to the Nigerian government between 1950 and 1972. First they steal your stuff and then they make you pay to get it back. Honestly, someone needs to civilise these Western savages.

The exhibit in the British Museum I like best is something else looted from Africa. The Shabako Stone, a relic from Ancient Egypt, is a 710-BC slab on to which an ancient scholar carved 60 vertical columns of hieroglyphs recording the Memphite Theology: the story of how the god Ptah brought all things into creation.

So far, so impressive.

Until someone found it lying around a few centuries later and decided it would make a really super millstone.

Can we pause to give this the attention it so richly deserves? You spend the best part of your adult life painstakingly, agonisingly, chiselling away at a piece of rock, so that the origins of the universe – the *origins of the universe* – are not forgotten. Only for some halfwit to come along and think: 'Hey, that's flat and solid! I'm gonna grind me some corn on this sucker.'

As a result, this ancient and holy tablet now has a whopping great hole in the middle and huge troughs scarring it from where this numbskull sawed away, humming blithely, never once stopping to consider: 'Wait a moment! In a world where a written alphabet is pretty novel, I'll bet these weird inscriptions could mean something interesting!'

Isn't that the ultimate illustration of the futility of human endeavour? It's pretty much the most depressing thing I've ever seen.

But this is why we need museums. To keep the Shabako Stones of the world safe and to remind us of the bad, as well as the good. In South Africa, we should have enough of both to fill countless thrilling museums.

14

Oscar Fever

I know more about Oscar Pistorius at this stage than I do about certain members of my own family. I have a better grip on the timeline of events at Pistorius's house on the night of February 13 2013 than I do on the entire history of human evolution. I am certain that my familiarity with the names and back-stories of various hangers-on in the Pistorius social circle has displaced far more significant information in my brain. Capital cities, for instance. I can no longer tell you the capital of Sudan, but I can draw you a detailed diagram to illustrate Oscar Pistorius's relationship history.

This is, obviously, a bit annoying, particularly given the fact that before Pistorius shot his girlfriend dead, I had no special interest in him. It was wonderful that he could run so fast on prosthetic legs. He clearly had had to overcome the kind of monumental obstacles that those of us who have two functioning legs can scarcely imagine.

At the same time, though, Pistorius was always able to benefit from lavish resources and powerful connections. I learnt from reading his ex-girlfriend's mother's account of their relationship that his Uncle Arnold's house – where Pistorius was shacked up for the duration of his murder trial – has a *lake*. That's pretty sweet, even by the standards of white South Africans.

Then there's the fact that Pistorius's place in the South African team at the London Olympics in 2012 was also won at the expense of sprint champion Simon Magakwe, who had faster qualifying times than Pistorius. There wasn't a lot of noise about this at the time because apparently so many people in the media and the sporting establishment were so enthralled by the Blade Runner narrative.

Magakwe said afterwards that his failure to be selected for the team had caused sponsors to lose interest in him. 'I feel very sad and hurt,' he said. He believed that if he had been able to benefit from the exposure of the Olympics: 'I would have been able to prepare for any competition without worrying about what my family was going to eat.' Maybe Uncle Arnold could find him a part-time job cleaning the lake.

After the shooting of Reeva Steenkamp, endless opinion pieces drew links between Pistorius's fall from grace and the failure of the so-called Rainbow Nation to live up to the shiny potential that beckoned in 1994. Truthfully speaking, I have cranked out far more tenuous pieces of analysis on the Pistorius case, but I never found this analogy particularly convincing.

It seems to imbue Pistorius's Paralympic success with a far wider significance and emotional resonance than was actually the case. I feel the same way when people talk about the 1995 Rugby World Cup as the greatest moment of unity the country has ever known because I'm convinced its impact was overhyped by white rugby fans and beer marketers.

In a preparatory phone chat for an interview with a US broadcaster, an American producer asked me please to sketch out the ways in which I felt Pistorius's fall mirrored the death of South African national hope. I replied that I didn't feel this to be the case. She didn't like that.

'I just wanna push back on that a little bit,' she said. I remained uncooperative. They never phoned me again.

On the opening day of the Pistorius trial, I agreed to do a live radio crossing for another international broadcaster.

'Many foreign journalists have reported being unnerved by the tabloidy relish that South African news outlets seem to be taking in this murder trial,' my host said, his voice coming down the line from London. 'Your comment on that, please.'

It's a good thing the medium was radio rather than TV because for a second my mouth actually dropped open with astonishment. It was the British tabloids that had descended like vultures on Pretoria in the days before the trial, tracking down Pistorius's alleged new girlfriend and smashing her face all over the cover of their newspapers after she was supposedly sold out by a classmate.

It was Sky News that 'obtained', in an unspecified way, CCTV footage of Steenkamp and Pistorius canoodling in a grocery store before the shooting, and a video of Pistorius blowing the shit out of a watermelon on a shooting range. It was Australia's Channel Seven that would later 'obtain' a re-enactment of the Pistorius shooting created as part of trial preparation by a private forensic company. When it came to taking a 'tabloidy relish' in the Pistorius trial, foreign journalists made the locals seem like amateurs.

'I just wanna push back on that a little,' I said to my radio host, or words to that effect. In the coming weeks I was especially aggrieved by his suggestion because there was a particular British radio correspondent who would sit in the courtroom bellowing his daily bulletins into his phone. Without fail, his account of what had happened in court that day would contain one or two outright lies. In fact, often listening to foreign correspondents deliver their pieces to camera at the day's end, I would wonder if we had been attending completely different trials.

'One of the reasons why you can cut the tension in this courtroom with a knife,' began one dashing foreign journalist, dramatically advancing towards the camera, 'is because the layout of the room forces the Steenkamp family and the Pistorius camp to sit literally shoulder to shoulder.'

At this point in the trial, the two groups were separated by *literally* about 10 metres. We developing world journalists could only watch and admire this gutsy disregard for the facts.

I spent many, many weeks sitting on the hard benches of courtroom GD of the North Gauteng High Court reporting on the Pistorius trial. It is not a period I shall look back on with unalloyed joy, though partly for reasons unconnected to the trial itself.

While in Pretoria I was staying in a hotel, in the loosest sense of the word. I quickly realised that what it amounted to was actually a tavern with rooms, like some form of medieval hostelry. There was little functional distinction between the lobby and the bar, and if I had lingered for a refreshing post-court beverage I had a strong suspicion that I would be assumed to be offering transactional sex.

Approaching the first morning of the trial, it was already clear that the media scrum would be fearsome and brutal. While places in the courtroom had been allocated to specific news outlets, seating would be decided *Lord of the Flies* style. Aware that I might never be able to leave my spot for fear of losing it, I concluded my hotel breakfast that morning by carefully wrapping two soggy muffins into serviettes to sustain me for the day.

In retrospect, these were unnecessary provisions, as I had already stuffed my backpack with enough snacks to last someone for a week on the Otter Trail. One couldn't be too careful, though. As I unzipped my bag to squeeze in the supplementary baked goods, a shadow loomed over me.

'I'm afraid you can't do that,' the manager said.

I protested that I had paid for a breakfast, and whether I ate the muffins at the table or in courtroom GD of the North Gauteng High Court seemed to make remarkably little difference to any affected parties. As I made my quite compelling case I blushed purple, however, because it is humiliating to be accused of stealing breakfast pastries.

He shook his head. I removed the muffins from my bag and replaced them on my plate. Then I trudged out of the restaurant. It wasn't a good start to Pretoria life.

The North Gauteng High Court is located in the city's centre, as was my so-called hotel. This is a world quite apart from Uncle Arnold's lake. Many parts of the city centre are run-down. There are massive potholes in the roads. As I made the 3-kilometre walk to and from the courtroom every day, I attracted some interested glances. I soon realised why: in all my weeks of walking, I never encountered another white person traversing the same route.

I did see a lot of white people driving past me, though. For the first three weeks of the trial, I think it rained every single day, heavily. That's how I remember it now, at any rate. As I walked the roads of central Pretoria, large cars swooshed by and, due to the poor drainage systems, they would drench me from head to toe. I stood, sodden, wiping water from my face like the nerd in a high-school movie. When that happened, I shook my fist at the sky and mouthed: Fuck you, Oscar.

To break up the tedium of my daily journey, there was a slight hint of danger on the streets. A fellow journalist had his phone taken from him at knifepoint a few roads from the courthouse. While I was walking to court one day, I made friendly eye contact with a man who was clearly criminally insane.

'Give me your phone!' he screamed at me. I shook my head grimly and quickened my pace.

'I have a gun and I will fucking shoot you!' he shouted. It seemed unlikely that he was telling the truth but I'd been covering the Pistorius trial for long enough to be persuaded that practically everyone in Pretoria has a gun.

At the trial's end, the elderly proprietor of the café I frequented near the courthouse told me that she, too, had a gun. I was taken aback because she was a 60-year-old tannie who wore her glasses on a chain around her neck.

'I carry it everywhere,' she said, patting the waistband of her elasticated trousers. 'And I'm a very good shot.'

Since the Jacaranda City seemed to be as awash with weaponry as a Brazilian favela, I was in no mood to risk finding out whether the man demanding my phone was bluffing. I took off. I started running, my backpack jiggling awkwardly on my shoulders. But to my indignation and horror, he had the same idea. He chased me down the road, yelling abuse. I was being pursued through the streets of central Pretoria by a madman, and it was *all Oscar Pistorius's fault.*

Eventually he gave up because he was too mad to be able to run and shout things at the same time. I arrived at the courtroom drenched in sweat, a change from arriving drenched in muddy, roadside water.

'What is it like, actually being in the courtroom?' people often asked me during the first weeks of the trial.

'Exactly the same as watching it from your couch, except we often can't hear as well as you on the couch,' I responded. This was partly true. If witnesses spoke softly you would see journalists bent forward in waves, trying to figure out what they were saying above the clatter of their neighbours' keyboards. The audio feed on the TV broadcast was way better.

But there were, of course, aspects of being actually present in the courtroom that you couldn't replicate at home. For one, the sight and sound of Oscar Pistorius vomiting into his green bucket. On those occasions I thanked the heavens that I'd chosen a seat on the other side of the courtroom because if I'd been closer to him I might have started sympathy-retching in response.

The judge was also strict about nobody making a noise, which was quite hard for me because I often had harsh, involuntary reactions to particularly thrilling moments of testimony. *What!* I would hiss. *Can you believe this shit?*

Then my friend Charl would jab me sternly with his elbow, and I'd recall that I was supposed to be a professional journalist, not somebody watching *Jersey Shore* with a mouthful of popcorn.

Charl and I were obsessed with making chilling eye contact with Pistorius. 'It just happened!' Charl would whisper, nudging me. 'Chilling eye contact with the accused!'

Making eye contact with Pistorius wasn't really chilling at all. We just put that bit in to make it seem more exciting. Most days Pistorius shuffled around the courtroom with a hangdog expression. Once he smiled at us and said, 'Good morning.'

'Good morning,' I muttered shyly back, smiling. I felt a bit star-struck, suddenly, and also quite charmed. Then I got a grip and remembered that he had killed someone, and also that he was currently ruining my life.

Driving to Johannesburg on the afternoon after the verdict, with Pretoria mercifully receding in the rear-view mirror, my colleague Jack turned to me.

'You want to hear another depressing thing?' he asked. (The first depressing thing, if it needs spelling out, was the verdict.)

'This has probably been the biggest story we'll ever cover in our lives.'

15

First World Problems

Air travel brings out the worst in me, and apparently in many other people as well. Terrorists, obviously, but also regular folk. A profound well of rage springs up in me in airports. Why do people walk so slowly and stupidly? Why can't anybody except me respect the queuing protocol?

The worst experience in this regard I've ever had was at Murtala Muhammed International Airport in Lagos. Far be it from me to tar an entire nation with one brush, but Nigerians are the world's most brazen and accomplished queue-jumpers. You'll be standing in the interminable check-in line in Lagos, and just as you're getting somewhere you'll discover that the man in front of you has been paid to keep the places of a family of approximately 45 individuals, who will languidly take up their positions directly ahead of you without displaying an ounce of personal shame.

I said absolutely nothing when this happened to me, needless to say, but I did shake my head in a disappointed manner.

I am a nervous traveller, which doesn't help. Not in terms of the actual flying. Though I did feel a prickle of anxiety on a tiny, rickety flight to Maputo once, when the Senegalese diplomat sitting next to me whipped out a rosary and began to pray extremely loudly. I wondered if he knew something I didn't.

No, what I mainly get nervous about is missing the flight, which has happened to me a few times. I once missed a flight from Johannesburg to Cape Town because I witnessed a scene at Wimpy that I found so touching that I started weeping uncontrollably and lost track of time.

There was an elderly white Afrikaans man at the counter, a few metres away from where I was seated. This being South Africa, obviously the elderly white man was in front of the counter, not behind it.

Having ordered his meal, he began to pat his pockets for his wallet.

'I can't find my wallet,' he said, with an edge of panic in his voice. 'I must have left it somewhere. I don't know where it is.'

'Sir, is it perhaps there?' asked the young black woman behind the counter, pointing at his breast pocket. It was indeed there. His level of relief seemed exaggerated, even given the inconvenience of potentially losing his wallet. He visibly sagged.

'I'm really sorry,' he said, his voice uneven. 'I was hijacked two weeks ago and I'm not coping very well.'

The young woman's face contorted in sympathy. 'What happened?' she asked gently.

He told her the harrowing tale. She responded with such warmth, such empathy, such *grace*, that I promptly burst into tears. I tried to cry inconspicuously, though, because naturally it wasn't great that I'd eavesdropped on their entire conversation.

'I will pray for you,' she ended, pressing his hand. He was clearly also deeply moved by her responses, although possibly not quite as much as me.

Then he left and I sat sobbing into my chicken mayo toastie, marvelling at the humanity still possible in insignificant interactions between normal

South Africans; the moments of beauty and goodness existing in their own perfect capsules, outside the history of our fractured land and the roles of oppressor and oppressed.

And while I was sobbing and marvelling, my flight left. Thanks a bunch, tortured old white man and saintly young black woman.

Missing a flight is infuriating because you generally have nobody to blame but yourself. But being bumped off a flight because it's overbooked, through no fault of your own, is almost equally maddening. This happens all the time on busy routes, but I'd never experienced it until recently – and I found the airline's way of dealing with the problem to be slightly surreal.

There were four of us who were bumped off the flight because we were the last to check in. The airline representative gathered us together and explained that we wouldn't be taking the flight we had booked. But, he said, he had two seats available on a flight three hours later. Two of us could have them. The other two would have to stay overnight and fly out the next morning.

'So you'll need to decide among yourselves who's taking the seats,' he said casually, and walked away.

Do you have any idea how excruciating it is to be faced with this complex social dilemma in a group of strangers? It was immediately apparent that all four of us were hungry for that next flight. Me and three young men.

'Okay, so we're gonna have to sort this out in a civilised way,' Young Man #1 said. He was travelling with his friend.

'Ja,' agreed his friend. 'Ching chong cha.'

This suggestion actually did not strike me as being particularly more unreasonable than any other, but his friend dismissed it with scorn.

'No, dude,' he said. 'We'll each go round and say why we need to catch the next flight.'

There was no indication how we would decide to award the spots on this basis. No criteria were laid out. Nobody had the authority over anyone else to judge the most compelling reason. But in the absence of any other plan, we went ahead.

What followed was an extremely awkward series of poignant speeches, probably mostly lies, as the three men attempted to outbid each other for the coveted spots. I hardly listened because my mind was racing. I actually had absolutely no good reason for why I needed to get home with such urgency. It was a Saturday evening. The only thing I was planning to do was get drunk with my friends. But I really, really wanted to get drunk with my friends.

I'm not proud to say that I instantly considered a number of outrageous lies. My mother's 70th birthday party. A sick child. A funeral. Wait – nobody has a funeral on a Saturday night. Scrap that.

I could see that the last dude was wrapping up. 'Blah blah lie lie blah home,' he was saying. He finished. All three turned to me.

I cried. Mysteriously, they were real tears. I was quite tired and I'd been reporting on the Pistorius case for some weeks, which had brought me to a state of slight existential despair. It is extremely embarrassing to cry in front of three strange men who are expecting you to account for yourself like a mature adult. Yet cry I did. I didn't say a single word.

Their expressions mixed pity, disgust and resignation. I knew exactly what they were thinking: 'For fuck's sake.'

'Well obviously *she's* got to have a seat,' Young Man #1 said, in a tone of ill-concealed resentment. I could understand why he was bitter. I was going to get a seat purely because I was a woman crying. I hadn't even told any of my lies. In normal life I have strong opinions about chivalry being incompatible with true gender equality, but there was a chilled bottle of Sauvignon Blanc with my name on it in Cape Town.

'Thank you,' I sniffled, and trotted away with my bag before they could change their minds.

I still find it bizarre, however, that the airline's chosen method of dealing with the problem was to force complete strangers into a torturous negotiation, as if we were part of a weird social experiment being observed by psychologists from behind a two-way mirror. Surely a more rational way of proceeding would have been to award the places according to the order in which people checked in?

But rationality often goes out the window in airports. They constitute quite a high-stress environment, even if you're on your way to a delightful holiday. I often find myself behaving in ways that would be alien to me elsewhere. All this crying, I should mention, is completely out of character for me. The other thing I do a lot of during air travel – and it truly shames me to admit this, as a hypocritical Best White – is racial profiling.

I was on a long-haul flight with my girlfriend two years ago when I began to notice that the man sitting next to me was behaving oddly. He seemed animated in a strange, aggressive fashion. He tapped his foot a lot. Sighed. Shook his head. I observed out of the corner of my eye that he was watching the Ben Affleck thriller *Argo*, which deals with the rescue of US diplomats from Iran during the 1979–1981 Iran hostage crisis.

Then something even more weird happened. *Argo* finished and he immediately pulled out the controls to his entertainment system and started the movie again. From the top. He had hundreds of other cinematic options at his disposal and he chose to watch the same movie *twice in a row*.

Why would anyone do this?

It had not escaped my attention that the man was dark skinned. His head was covered. I became seized with the possibility that he was watching *Argo* on repeat to get into the mood for jihad. The film had been criticised for its stereotyped, Islamophobic depiction of Iranians.

Let me pause to point out the obvious: what was going on here was sheer, unadulterated racism. On the flimsiest possible evidence – that this man was dark skinned, covered his head, seemed a bit pissed off and watched *Argo* twice in quick succession – I was actually contemplating the possibility that he might be a terrorist. If all of the above had applied, except that he had been white instead of dark skinned, the thought would probably never have crossed my mind.

There is absolutely no excuse for it. My life has not been touched by terror attacks, except in one relatively weak way. I woke up in London on the morning of July 7 2005, ready to take a tube to the airport, and turned on the TV to find that bombs had gone off on three underground trains and a bus, killing 57 and injuring 700. At that stage there was no way of knowing if there would be further explosions, but it seemed entirely likely. I had to get to the airport and I couldn't afford to take a taxi. Getting on a bus that morning felt like the most frightening thing I had ever done. My knees were shaking and as I gripped the handrail I prayed to a God I didn't believe in that the bus would not blow up.

But it didn't. No harm came to me whatsoever. And yet here I was, sitting on a plane, wallowing in my own prejudice.

The man next to me paused *Argo* and pressed the little button that summons the flight attendant. I sat rigidly. She arrived.

'Can I have some red wine, please?' he asked politely.

Relief, instantly followed by shame, flooded me. He obviously was not about to unleash holy war on the plane if he was settling in for a dop. Considered in this light, watching *Argo* twice in a row while hating every second suddenly seemed perfectly harmless. Maybe he was an aggrieved film critic? Maybe he was a disgruntled Iranian historian fuming over the film's inaccuracies and working up an op-ed piece in his head? Maybe I should seek help for my latent bigotry?

There's just something about planes that seems to turn me into the kind of person most often found in a Fox News studio, though. At the height of the Ebola outbreak in 2014, with the virus ravaging West Africa, I flew from Cape Town to London. The man sitting next to me, who I knew to be Nigerian because he'd told the woman seated on the other side, made a phone call moments before we took off.

'I am feeling a bit better,' he said, coughing. I spent 13 hours contemplating my Ebola funeral.

16

A Royal Encounter

I went to Buckingham Palace once to meet the Queen. Trust me, if I could think of a more suave manner in which to bring this up, I would. I spend a lot of time trying to think of a way to drop it casually into conversation. It's extraordinarily difficult to do so without seeming either like a massive wanker or someone who has a cultish reverence for the British Royal Family. And without meaning to seem ungrateful for Her Majesty's hospitality, I do think they are basically ... unnecessary.

I once met someone who had a much better Royal Family anecdote than mine. She had been to a wedding at which Princes Harry and William were both in attendance, and she claimed William got sullenly drunk and kissed a number of girls who were not Kate Middleton. They weren't married yet, I should add, and I should further add that this story is completely unverifiable. (Does that constitute a legal disclaimer?)

The morning after I'd been to Buckingham Palace, I stumbled out of my bedroom in a London house I was sharing with two boys and ran into a strange woman who appeared to have spent the night.

'Hello,' I croaked, trying to unglue my eyelids.

'Hello,' she said, eyeing me with visible concern.

'I'm so sorry,' I whispered hoarsely, gripping the staircase for support. 'I'm just so terribly hungover.'

'Oh, okay!' she said brightly. 'Why, where were you last night?'

I paused. The universe stood still for a moment.

'Buckingham Palace,' I mumbled, unable to make eye contact. 'The Queen had a ... thing.'

'Riiiiight,' she said. She said it in a tone I instantly recognised because it was *exactly* the same tone that I used on a strange man on a bus once when he told me that he invented bungee jumping. (I went home and looked him up, because he had pressed his business card into my hand, and found out that he *did* invent bungee jumping!)

'Anyway, nice to meet you,' she said, and walked into the lounge. She wasn't actually twirling her finger against her temple as she walked away, but she might as well have been.

I stared after her helplessly. *She thinks I am a deranged liar*, I thought. *She thinks that this is my crazy make-believe for the day, but that tomorrow I'll have moved on to claim that Lindsay Lohan is my first cousin, or that my dad invented the fax machine, or something.*

Maybe I should go after her, I thought. *Maybe I should follow her into that room and convince her I am telling the truth by showing her my invitation, on thick, embossed, ivory card, with the royal insignia. Or I could ask her to smell my hand, to see if there isn't maybe the tiniest whiff of powdered glove on it.*

I did nothing of the kind, however, because I was in danger of vomiting.

Allow me to clarify a point that may have you confused: I doubt that the Queen was similarly indisposed that morning. I did not receive any SMSes from her, for instance, saying, 'Am sooooooo hungover LOL wtf did we do last nite????? Don't u dare tag me in any pix on Facebook u biatch!!'

Her Majesty did not hand around flaming sambucas or lead us in a round of 'how low can you go', or dare people to down their drink quicker than her.

In fact, I did not see a drop of alcohol slip down her royal throat, which was a bit irksome to contemplate the morning after. Like when a teetotaller friend invites you round for dinner and you end up getting disgracefully drunk and then she phones you the next morning, poison dripping from every syllable, to say, 'How's the head?'

In fairness, it was not at the Palace itself that the major descent into inebriation occurred, but afterwards. Afterwards, when we spilled like laughing children out into the rainy London evening, euphoric with reflected glory, sprinkled with the fairy dust of proximity to ancient power – it was then that we decided it might be nice to round off the evening with 14 pints at the closest dive-bar. It only seemed fitting.

But before I get ahead of myself, the question that may understandably be foremost on your mind at this point is: 'Why on earth were you – *you!* – invited to Buckingham Palace?' The most plausible answer to that is 'an administrative error'. I had to borrow *shoes*, for God's sake. And a handbag. That is probably not a situation that most visitors to Buckingham Palace normally find themselves in.

It was 2010 and Her Maj was about to host President Jacob Zuma for a state visit. In advance of that, she threw a reception for South Africans in the UK. I had been working for a networking organisation dealing with that precise demographic and had assisted the Palace with some contact details. Either due to the aforementioned error, or out of pity, or because they simply have *awfully good manners*, they chucked an invitation my way too.

I do not recall the Palace security measures as being particularly onerous. In fact, I have been more rigorously searched at the Chamber of Mines in Johannesburg. We weren't allowed to take our cellphones in, though. This was obviously devastating, since what is the bloody point of going to

Buckingham Palace if you can't have some kind of lewd selfie on a throne?

There were matching his-'n'-hers pink thrones, by the way. The Queen's was embroidered with the ERII heraldry, and Prince Philip's with a simple 'P'. They were, in a word, kitsch.

The Palace toilet paper is *not*, contrary to what you may have thought, embossed with any royal logo. Just as well, or whole rolls of it would have ended up in my borrowed handbag. *You need to steal something with logo*, my friend Cristina informed me sternly in advance of my visit. *Anything with logo.* But there was nothing with logo, other than the thrones, which would have presented difficulties to smuggle out.

Shortly after I had cased the joint for thievable merchandise, we were shepherded into a line like feudal serfs to be introduced to Elizabeth II. As you advanced upon the monarch, a court functionary intoned your name and designation.

I had been instructed in advance that to *squeeze* the Queen's hand was a treasonous no-no. Naturally, I went too far in the opposite direction: by laying my sweaty palm in her glove with the softest of touches and withdrawing it immediately, like the old 'too slow', faux high five.

To compensate I went on to crunch Prince Philip's hand as if we were engaged in an arm-wrestling competition, and then lingered in the hope that he would deliver some racist non-sequitur to me that I could sell to the papers. Something like 'South African, eh? And yet not a blackie. Extraordinary.' Instead of which he beamed at me perfectly benevolently and politically correctly and I felt ashamed.

When we had paid our respects in this fashion, we proceeded to a large reception room. Waiters whisked past with endless champagne flutes. The Queen made her way from one conversational group to the next, never lingering for more than about two minutes.

When she reached us, some grizzled old expat seized his chance.

'And have you been to South Africa, Your Majesty?' he asked. Not the most intelligent of questions, since the woman is *the head of the Commonwealth.*

She took it well. Perhaps she hears similar things from Prince Philip every day over breakfast.

'Oh yes,' she said. 'I visited for the first time in 1947.'

And then she said something that sounded extraordinarily sincere and oddly personal.

'I remember horse-riding with my sister on the beach,' she said. 'I don't think I've ever felt so free.'

It struck me as a moment of exquisite poignancy. Can you feel sorry for a woman born into unfathomable wealth and power? I think you can, when the trade-off has been any semblance of a normal life. For a second, with all the trappings of her gilded cage stripped away, she seemed both vulnerable and *old*. I experienced a sudden surge of affection for this short, hunched, white-haired lady.

When the Queen unobtrusively made her exit, a certain excited frisson to the environment evaporated, but it was replaced with a kind of relief, like being released from the headmistress's office. I got properly stuck into the champagne.

At the boozy tail end of the evening, after cornering singer Annie Lennox in a way I do not care to recall, I met the management accountant of the Royal Household. She was an Afrikaans woman from the Klein Karoo, with an accent so thick and warm I wanted to spread it on my toast. She had weekly one-on-ones with the Queen, she told me, where the Queen pores over the figures for all her properties with steely vigilance, alert to sudden upturns in the quantity of dishwashing liquid purchased for Balmoral or the amount of lamb chunks for the corgis they're going through at Windsor.

'And you know the thing about the Queen?' she said earnestly. 'She don't take shit, hey.'

With those words echoing, her colleague gently but firmly began to usher us towards the Palace doors.

17

Mansplain that to Me Again

My girlfriend Jeanine and I were once at a drinks party, where we were introduced to a man we'd never met. I'll call him Ross. It was 2012, shortly before the ANC's elective congress at Mangaung, which was very much on our minds – since I am a journalist and Jeanine helps run a TV newsroom.

Someone else present brought up the congress and asked what its date was.

'The 16th of December, I think,' Jeanine responded.

Ross turned to her. 'Mangaung is the ANC's elective congress,' he said helpfully. 'It's where they decide who the party leaders will be.'

Jeanine and I looked at each other in sheer bemusement. She had been introduced as someone working in news management. She had answered a question about Mangaung seconds earlier, displaying a clear familiarity with the subject. So why was a *wine salesman* lecturing a *news editor* about the biggest political story in South Africa that year?

Sound your 'mansplaining' klaxon, dear friends!

The person credited with first sketching out the concept behind mansplaining was writer Rebecca Solnit – though she didn't invent the term itself. Solnit was introduced to a wealthy man at a party in Aspen who asked her, 'in the way you encourage your friend's seven-year-old to describe flute practice', to tell him what her books were about.

She explained that she had just written a book on Eadward Muybridge, the 19th-century English photographer who developed a device that paved the way for modern cinematography.

The man cut her off. 'Have you heard about the *very important* Muybridge book that came out this year?' She and her friend tried to explain that Solnit was, in fact, the author of the book. He paid no attention, waxing lyrical about this far superior book she should be familiar with. Solnit's friend had to say 'That's her book' three or four times before the information penetrated.

This dude was attempting to lecture her on a book *she had actually written.*

In an essay on the subject, Solnit records: 'That I was indeed the author of the very important book it turned out he hadn't read, just read about in *The New York Times Book Review* a few months earlier, so confused the neat categories into which his world was sorted that he was stunned speechless – for a moment, before he began holding forth again.'

Solnit's essay was published in 2008, and since then the term 'mansplaining' has been in common use to describe a scenario when a man takes it upon himself to explain a subject to a woman with the assumption that the woman cannot possibly have the same degree of knowledge on the matter as a man.

In my experience, many men – even men who are in other respects deeply sensitive to gender inequality – find 'mansplaining' an irritating term. There *are* occasions on which an individual man's knowledge of a subject will outstrip a woman's, they protest. Can a man *never* display superior knowledge of a subject? Mansplaining is not *always* done in a patronising way, they plead. Some *women* do exactly the same thing. And beyond this, some people are just arseholes, who take every opportunity to show off their knowledge regardless of the listener. It's not necessarily a gender thing.

Yeah, yeah, yeah.

I accept all of those in certain contexts but I think they can be red herrings. Of course not all men are mansplainers. Calm down there, dudes. But so many women I know experience some form of mansplaining so frequently that you'll have to work a lot harder on convincing me that it's not a legitimate thing.

I got talking about it recently at a dinner with friends. One, who is a Cambridge-educated historian, said she has had male taxi drivers attempt to explain her highly niche research area to her. Taxi drivers seem to be common offenders. I'd been in Parliament listening to a plenary debate on the Marikana massacre, when I took a taxi home. My male driver asked me about myself, and I explained that I was a journalist and that I was in Parliament for the Marikana debate.

He soon realised that I'd got the wrong idea about what happened at Marikana, where 34 striking mineworkers were shot dead by police in August of 2012. He said the police acted entirely in self-defence. I accepted that we might have a difference of opinion – that is distinct from a mansplaining issue – but he proceeded to correct me on points of fact.

'The Farlam Commission heard that most of the miners were shot in the back,' I said mildly.

'No, no, my dear,' he said kindly. 'Not at all. Those people had violence in their hearts.'

Was he just a stubborn individual who refused to relinquish his cherished version of the world? Maybe. But would he have told a male journalist that he was wrong about the facts in the same way? I'm not sure. And I know for certain that he would never have called a male journalist 'my dear'.

Another friend, an experienced journalist for a business publication, was recently preparing to carry out an interview. A male admin assistant – a man with not a day's training in journalism in his life – intervened to deliver some handy hints before she left.

'I think you'll find that what works best is if you ask open-ended questions, not ones that can be answered with yes or no,' he advised.

Was this man just some insanely annoying know-it-all with limited social skills, someone like the David Brent character in the British version of the sitcom *The Office*? Perhaps. But again, the point is that he was not dispensing the same kind of guidance to her male colleagues.

Women with technical knowledge in various fields get mansplained to endlessly. A friend who is a professional videographer once had a blacksmith explain to her what lenses she should be using. Another, a video editor, describes the hell that is dealing with salesmen and parts suppliers who always begin by assuming she knows absolutely nothing about the specialised equipment she has expressed an interest in.

There also appears to be a major mansplaining issue around driving, unsurprisingly.

'You aren't comfortable driving a manual car, are you,' a male employee commented to my female friend, who happened to be his boss. The man also happened to *not* have a driver's licence or, in fact, any experience of driving whatsoever.

Telling me this story, my friend adds: 'By the way, I could drive one of those jeeps used for desert warfare. I could drive a *fucking tank.*'

A lawyer friend having a recent conversation about the Pistorius case was repeatedly told by a male financial analyst: 'Yes, but you must also remember, in our legal system ...' He was fully aware of her two law degrees. My friend reports: 'At the end of the conversation, knowing I'm a lawyer, he said: "I like you. You think like a lawyer."'

Another friend was at a tea party the other day and got into a conversation about someone not present who had a doctorate from Yale.

A male high school student – a *high school student* – turned to her and explained charitably: 'Yale is, like, one of the best universities in the United States. It's part of what is called the "Ivy League", like Oxford or Cambridge, those famous universities in England.'

My friend nodded politely. She has a doctorate from Oxford and has done fellowships at two Ivy League universities.

These are just a few of the experiences of women I personally know. There's a website (mansplained.tumblr.com) to which women submit their accounts of mansplaining. These submissions come in at such a volume that the website administrators frequently publish more than one post per day.

'Today at work (restaurant) this bartender told me he's been to Turkey five times, and that I say "hello" wrong in Turkish. I'm Turkish.'

And my favourite, where a woman actually had *her own breasts* mansplained to her by a stranger: 'At a popular lingerie store, I asked for assistance in the general vicinity of another young lady and the gentleman accompanying her. I pointed out the style I'd like and told the salesperson my size – a 32DD. The young man, at this point, turned and walked towards me and stated, "No, you're not a DD. Those are too small to be that size. You're a C or something".'

But of course, women could just be misinterpreting this stuff, because we're insecure and hypersensitive. What we really need round here is a man to explain to us why mansplaining isn't a thing.

18

Tattoo or Not Tattoo?

Did you know that if you get struck by lightning, you can end up with a tattoo?

Getting struck by lightning is obviously less than desirable. I read an interview once with a guy who got struck and he said it felt like 'someone punched me in the back of my head'. Interestingly, he reported that it wasn't burny at all. He just felt like he'd been knocked out. Although directly afterwards he went back to playing a game of volleyball, which seems an unusual response.

The tattoos you can end up with, however, are exceptionally striking. They're called Lichtenburg figures, and they resemble tribal markings: they are literally burnt into your skin. They are amazing to look at in photos. In some cases they have a delicate frond pattern; in other cases they look pretty much exactly like what you'd imagine you'd get if you walked into an extremely talented tattoo artist's parlour and requested a tattoo of lightning.

I don't have any tattoos because I can't think of any particular word or image that I can commit to treasuring for the rest of my life. I think a lot of people have the same problem. My friend Adam once told me that the only thing he might consider was a tattoo of an apple. Not the tech company, an actual apple. He said he felt confident that he would always love apples.

I understood his reasoning, but the obvious flaw in our current era is that everyone would assume it was some kind of ironic statement on the tech company.

I get anxious thinking about the people who get whimsical tattoos in the flush of youth, or inebriation, and then spend the next decade hating the sight of their own skin. The worst tattoo I've ever seen in real life was on the local drunkard in a village in the Scottish Highlands. When he described it to me I didn't believe him, so he obligingly stripped off his shirt to show me.

He'd lost a bet, you see, and the penalty was that he had to allow his friend to tattoo his back with a needle strapped to a vibrator. His friend was clearly a terrifying sadist, because the artwork he'd chosen to create on Danny's back took the form of three giant, squiggly words: 'Bobby Woz Here'.

I wonder if he still has that tattoo and what women think of it when he disrobes for the first time. I imagine they'd get a faint whiff of *eau de prison*.

There was obviously an element of duress in Danny's tattoo experience. But there's actually a psychological theory to explain why people get such reckless tattoos in other contexts. It's called the 'end-of-history illusion', and it refers to the misconception people have that even though they have changed an enormous amount up to the present moment, they will not continue to change in the future.

Our past selves? Ja, they were different and weird. But our future selves will be exactly the same as they are today.

This delusion affects people of all ages and intelligence. In one study, a team of Harvard psychologists asked people how much they would be willing to pay today to see their favourite band from a decade ago perform. Then they asked them how much they'd pay in ten years' time to see their current favourite band play. Invariably, they were willing to shell out loads more for the latter. Though their best band ten years ago now didn't seem worth forking out very much for, they were confident that they'd still feel the same passion in a decade's time for the music they loved now.

'Believing that we just reached the peak of our personal evolution makes us feel good,' one researcher explained.

It's an understandable fallacy, though I feel tattoo parlours should have some kind of pre-counselling where they ask you if you might potentially be in the grip of the end-of-history illusion. Of course, the problem is that you'd always answer no.

My girlfriend Jeanine has several tattoos, some of which I am fond and some of which I am slightly less fond. She got her first tattoo at age 16 when she set out for a parlour with a friend and R40 burning a hole in her pocket.

(It strikes me as strange, incidentally, that the term for the dingily lit establishments you enter to get your flesh permanently branded with coloured ink is a 'parlour'. It sounds much too genteel. They should call it something more appropriate, like a 'lair'.)

For R40 at a Pretoria tattoo parlour in the 1990s you had two choices: a rose or a spider. Not being much of a rose girl, Jeanine opted for the spider. I still cannot imagine why you would be charmed by the idea of an arachnid stencilled as crawling out of your pants, but that end-of-history illusion is a real fucker.

A decade or so later, Jeanine decided it was time for her and her spidery little pal to call it a day. Tattoo removal is tricky and expensive, so she opted to cover it with another tattoo instead. It's a sort of abstract spirally pattern. It kind of *had* to be an abstract spirally pattern, since the only thing that would perfectly cover a spider and its eight little legs would be another spider.

As far as solutions go, it's not bad. I have been wondering recently what route former England cricketer Kevin Pietersen is planning to take out of his own tattoo problem.

Pietersen, who is originally South African, attracted a lot of criticism for his decision to play for England instead. In 2005 he announced that he was unveiling the ultimate proof of his new allegiance: a massive tattoo of England's 'three lions' symbol.

'That's not a Christmas present, that's for life,' he said at the time.

Fast-forward eight years, with Pietersen dropped from the England team after a string of controversies, and he releases an autobiography in which he says he regrets the tattoo and has realised that South Africa is his 'real home'.

Well, *that's* awkward.

I don't know what Pietersen has planned. With some inventive antler placement and a tail dock, perhaps he could turn the lions into springboks.

When American writer David Foster Wallace met fellow writer Mary Karr, he got a tattoo of a heart with her name in it. Then they broke up. For almost a decade, Foster Wallace seems to have wandered around with Mary's imprint on him. I can't imagine what you'd tell subsequent girlfriends, who surely wouldn't be thrilled. Maybe he didn't date very much, though he did once speculate that his purpose on Earth was to 'put my penis in as many vaginas as possible'.

A full nine years later, he fell in love with another woman, artist Karen Green. The force of his feelings for Green seems to have finally galvanised him into some tattoo-related action. Or maybe Karen put her foot down.

He chose an unusual method of dealing with the issue, though. He had a tattoo artist draw a line through Mary's name and put an asterisk under the heart. Further down his arm, he then had another asterisk tattooed – with Karen's name.

Like this, it seems:

Mary*

*Karen

I really don't know how I'd feel about that, if I were Karen. If he didn't want to remove the Mary heart, he could've just got an abstract spirally pattern over it, or a springbok. Foster Wallace's books are famously packed with dense footnotes, but it seems a kind of wanky way to make some postmodern literary point.

I prefer actor Johnny Depp's way out of a similar conundrum. Depp had 'Winona Forever' tattooed on his arm when he was engaged to fellow celebrity Winona Ryder. It seems that having someone's name inked on you is basically a cosmic guarantee that your relationship will fail, and fail it did. But Depp didn't want to erase the tattoo because that would be 'to try and say it never happened', he told GQ in 1993.

At the time of the interview, he was considering various modifications. 'If I alter it in some way, make it funny – put her next boyfriend's name on top of it, say – it would still be honest,' he mused.

Put her next boyfriend's name on top of it? For a *joke*? What is this guy, a moron? Thankfully sense prevailed and he got the tattoo changed to read 'Wino Forever' instead.

Depp was just really lucky that his ex-girlfriend had a name that you could modify through the removal of two letters to form a valid though unflattering identity marker for yourself. That doesn't happen every day. If he'd been dating Salma Hayek he probably would have had to change it to Salmon.

If you had a lightning tattoo instead of a regular ink one you'd never have to worry about any of this shit, because the markings of electrostatic discharge have a timeless elegance. The other obvious advantage is the absolutely superb pick-up line it would present.

'Cool tattoo,' some Cape Town hipster would croon at you in a bar. 'Who did it for you?'

And then you'd take a deep slug of your craft beer and reply, 'Nature.'

19

A Match Made in Hell

I have an unshakeable curiosity to visit North Korea. Don't get me wrong. I'm sure it wouldn't exactly be a Disney cruise. In my mind North Korea is sort of like the Ice Kingdom of Narnia because I've only ever seen pictures of it where it looks eternally wintry, with ordinary North Koreans being lashed by wind and snow while their leaders parade around snugly in those furry hats that the Soviets are so fond of.

I know that the weather can't be bad all the time, though, because the country is so often ravaged by drought. So logically speaking they must have quite a lot of nice sunny days.

It's easier to visit North Korea now than it used to be, though if you're a journalist, things are still a bit sticky. You get marshalled from one national shrine to the next by hyper-vigilant minders, stopping only to genuflect and lay flowers. A bit like what I'd imagine a school trip to the Taal Monument must've been like during apartheid.

The one thing counting in your favour as a prospective South African visitor to North Korea is your nationality, since the two countries are still basically besties.

It's a funny thing, that.

Did you ever have a friend in high school who was all nice and normal, but in the decade or so after leaving school went on to become a massive wankstain, and you felt like you couldn't unfriend them on Facebook because, well, history?

I feel that this has a bit of a resemblance to what South Africa's relationship with North Korea is like. The analogy breaks down on a number of levels when you look at it closely, most obviously that North Korea has never been particularly nice and normal, but bear with me.

North Korea helped the ANC during the armed struggle by training guerrillas, and also apparently sent over a shit-ton of people to fight in the Angolan Civil War. So it's understandable that the ANC government kinda feels like it owes them.

But it's also massively counter-intuitive that a government which fought for the liberation of its population would be on WhatsApp terms with a country that has sent hundreds of thousands of people to labour camps and makes them eat rats.

If you want to know what North Korean labour camps are like, you should read *Escape from Camp 14*, the account of a North Korean defector born in one of the camps, who told his story to an American journalist. In early 2015 it was revealed that there were inaccuracies with the timeline of the defector's narrative, but the chronicle of camp life is harrowing enough: Shin Dong-hyuk's mother and brother were executed in front of him after he betrayed them in the hope of getting more food.

And when I say 'more food', by the way, what I really mean is 'food'.

But to make it worse, when this dude eventually escaped to America, everyone expected him to spend the rest of his life addressing human rights groups when all he wanted to do was sit around and eat noodles.

And who can blame him? If I had escaped from a North Korean prison camp, I would definitely take that as a justification to spend the rest of my natural life bingeing on reality TV and family packs of KitKats.

'I still think of freedom as roasted chicken,' he once mused in an interview.

As various experts on North Korea have pointed out, there is less space to question government in North Korea than there was even in the darkest days of apartheid South Africa: no unions, no churches, no protest marches. But democratic South Africa seems happy to write off this quality in its old pal as some sort of charming quirk.

The West has been bugging South Africa for yonks to use its BFF status with North Korea to get the country to give up its nuclear weapons. We're actually perfectly placed to make the case because South Africa is one of only four countries ever to give up its nuclear weapons voluntarily, in 1990.

One of the others was Ukraine, but in 2014 Ukrainian President Petro Poroshenko said they'd made a terrible mistake. He said they'd fallen into the trap of 'believing the world had all turned vegetarian', which is an interesting way of putting it.

I didn't actually know until recently that South Africa ever had any nuclear weapons. Nor did many other people at the time, since the government sort of kept it on the down-low. Understandably, since the international community tends to get a bit twitchy when you start bragging about your nukes. But what's the point of having nuclear weapons if you never tell anyone about them so they can fear and demonise you? It seems to take some of the fun out of it.

It was only in 1993 that FW de Klerk dropped the official word to Parliament that South Africa had ditched the nuclear weapons many people didn't know for certain had existed three years earlier.

The plan had been one of 'strategic ambiguity' previously: we will neither admit nor deny having nuclear weapons. I don't know why more countries don't just adopt a policy of infuriating vagueness as to whether or not they have nuclear weapons instead of embarking on the costly exercise of actually bothering to enrich uranium.

'Lesotho! Do you have nuclear weapons?'

'Mayyybee! Maybe not!', with a coy wink, when the UN gets on your ass. It's not even technically a lie.

In 1990 De Klerk decided to dismantle the nuclear weapons. In fairness, it must have taken about 15 minutes, since they only had six. A lot of people subsequently fawned over South Africa and its commitment to international harmony, but it's been suggested that a less awesome reason for nuclear disarmament was that De Klerk and the government of the day didn't want those black terrorists to get their hands on nukes when they came to power.

I don't know about you, but this suggestion has the distinct ring of truth to me.

Since 2006, South Africa *has* been gently hinting that North Korea should ditch its nuclear weapons. Pretoria also told on North Korea to the United Nations in 2010. North Korea, it emerged, was sending containers of tank parts and military equipment to the Democratic Republic of Congo, via good old Durban. To disguise the parts, they were concealed amidst sacks of rice. We know this from the terse South African report on the matter to the UN. But then, on the shipping documents, North Korea wrote that the cargo was 'bulldozer parts'.

I mean, find one story and stick to it! If it's a skip full of bulldozer parts, why is there half a rice paddy in there too?

That's not the kind of thing that gets past our eagle-eyed customs inspectors. North Korea might as well have stuck the parts in an envelope and labelled it 'Gift – socks. Approx value R50', the way the rest of us do.

We confiscated the hell out of those parts and ratted out North Korea. They can't have been thrilled about that. But there's no indication that it irrevocably soured the bromance.

In 2013 Deputy Minister of International Relations and Cooperation

Ebrahim Ebrahim visited the capital Pyongyang. When the *Daily Maverick* asked him why, after the trip, he said – along with other stuff, admittedly – 'They kept inviting us.'

Well, we all know how awkward that can get. That precise scenario has led me into many of the most unpleasant social experiences of my life.

Ebrahim said that Pyongyang was 'very clean', which isn't a shocker considering it is reportedly treated like a set from *The Truman Show*, with its pavements washed by hand and the roadside grass cut with scissors. If true, that is a job creation scheme and a half.

He did complain, however, about the quality of food at their hotel. 'Breakfast was not a buffet,' he said. 'You get a yoghurt and two slices of toast, that's all.'

That's a yoghurt and two slices of toast more than they're getting in the labour camps, Mr Ebrahim, but I do appreciate how disappointing a meagre hotel breakfast can be. A good one really sets you up for the day.

It isn't only the South African government that are North Korea fans. There's a special group called the South African Association of Friendship and Solidarity with Korean People that meets up regularly in Mpumalanga to praise the good works of Pyongyang. They claim to have at least 1 600 members.

I interviewed their leader, Boniface Majuba, a few years ago. He, too, had been on a sponsored jolly to Pyongyang and seemed to have had a blast.

'When I was there I saw the people of North Korea living nicely,' he told me.

I was reminded, ironically, of the amount of money spent by the apartheid government on international propaganda campaigns. At its peak, it was believed to be spending around $100 million per year on improving its international image. Unbelievably, one of the tactics was to target African Americans. US journalist Ron Nixon's *Operation Blackwash: Apartheid South Africa's 46-year Propaganda War on Black America* tells the story.

After the Soweto Uprising in 1976, the apartheid regime contracted a black American named Robert T Hatcher to handle the government's escalating PR nightmare in the US. Hatcher encouraged black business to invest in South Africa and set up trips to the country for suitable black American legislators and journalists who could report back on how they'd seen 'the people of South Africa living nicely', essentially.

Leaders of the ANC Youth League, too, have been on a number of Pyongyang junkets. They may have been drunk at the time, or all the time. Erstwhile Youth League leader Floyd Shivambu – now ripping it up in Parliament with the Economic Freedom Fighters – enquired in 2010: 'Who says that North Korea is pursuing nuclear weapons?'

Um … North Korea says that. Continuously. That lovable scamp Kim Jong-Un has warned both the US and South Korea of 'deadly nuclear catastrophe' coming their way.

But ANC Youth League political tuition seems to take place over a nyaope pipe. When former leader Kim Jong-il died in 2011, the Youth League paid effusive tribute to a man who had, they said, devised 'an air steriliser to curb emission and related hazards from the climate'.

If only they would look at curbing their own emissions.

It's unclear what would have to happen in order for South Africa to stop sexting North Korea. There are satellite images of the prison camps and Pyongyang has admitted that 'labour detention camps' exist. There are the chilling accounts of multiple defectors. A 400-page United Nations investigation into human rights abuses in North Korea in 2014 compared the situation to the 'great scourges' of Nazism, apartheid and the Khmer Rouge.

North Korea's state news agency responded by pointing to the report's author's '40-odd-year-long career of homosexuality'. Since playground logic seems to be the order of the day, maybe the South African government is afraid of being called gay too. But it seems like a small price to pay to avoid being on the wrong side of history yet again.

20

A Stitch in Time Saves Nine

It used to be that when people said 'Notice anything different?' and looked at me expectantly, they'd be referring to an edgy haircut or a significant eyebrow pluck. Nowadays, they accompany the question with a meaningful forehead tap. Botox.

Oh Time, you old joker.

Botox is probably within my own future too, to be honest. When I concentrate on a task – such as writing – my face crunches into a maniacal rictus that is sometimes mistaken for mirth, though it's actually an expression of deep pain. Because of continuously screwing up my visage in this way, at the age of 32 I have already developed facial corrugations that are starting to trace their way from my eyes to my ears.

I don't mind those so much, since I think crinkly wrinkles around your eyes can make you look friendly, like a bulldog. What I do mind are the two grim furrows that are carving themselves from the sides of my nose down to my chin like First World War trenches, giving my face in repose a perpetual air of bitter disapproval.

This is, I assume, why strange men so often tell me to 'cheer up', or 'smile' because it 'can't be that bad'.

When this happens, it oddly fails to get me in the mood to crack out a jolly grin.

'Actually, it *is* that bad,' I want to reply. 'My entire family has Ebola and we have been hounded from our village.'

Fortunately, the *Daily Mail* is continuously on hand to explain to women like me exactly what's wrong with us. 'Bitchy Resting Face, when a woman looks "thoughtfully sad or angry for no reason", has been confirmed by experts as a very real phenomenon,' ran a July 2013 article.

Then they quoted a plastic surgeon who said we must all immediately have a 'grin lift', used to 'turn a permanent frown upside down'.

What does that even mean? I certainly don't want my face screwed into a perpetual smile. Apart from the obviously inappropriate potential – smirking your way through a funeral – everyone would always assume that you were delighted by their company. I can't think of anything worse.

So I won't be treating myself to a grin lift any time soon. If my face continues its interesting trajectory, however, I will end up with friendly bulldog eyes and a venomous hag mouth. I'm not totally averse to this idea – party on the top, vengeance on the bottom – but I'm pretty sure that at some point I'm going to surrender to the lure of a needle.

Does this make me a terrible feminist? Conveniently enough, I'm not sure it does. I'm not convinced that being a true feminist means you just have to put up with your face looking more and more like it was carved out of the side of Table Mountain. Why would it mean this?

You can, of course, deplore the social pressures brought to bear on women to keep looking young and fresh. I certainly am deploring them. I am deploring myself for being so feeble-minded that I have internalised all these damaging cultural messages. I am also deploring the double standard that sees visibly aged men still celebrated and filmed and invited to parties, while visibly aged women are basically asked please to cover their heads with a plastic bag and walk out into the wilderness to die.

I exaggerate somewhat, of course. If you are a certain kind of British character actress (see: Judi Dench; Helen Mirren; that other one), you are allowed to age in public. In Judi Dench's case, I suspect this may be because she was actually born 55 – have you ever seen a photo of a young Judi Dench?

This special dispensation looks set to be extended to Meryl Streep, too. If she could adopt a posh English accent in her old age, that would be helpful, so as not to confuse things.

Of all the many ridiculous articles I have written for women's magazines, possibly the most absurd was one claiming that women in their 60s and 70s were now the new 'silver foxes' of Hollywood, all-powerful and desired. (I mentioned Judi Dench, Helen Mirren, and that other one.) The phrase 'sexy septuagenarian' definitely featured.

As much as I'd love this to be true, I don't think it is – though I believe that it might be easier being an old actress in Hollywood than a middle-aged one. That's when you're truly invisible, I suspect, even though it must be said that contemporary television dramas are much better at juicy and interesting roles for middle-aged women.

Movies, not so much. There's that classic line from *The First Wives Club*: 'There are only three ages for women in Hollywood: Babe, District Attorney and Driving Ms Daisy.' And the District Attorney roles are probably thinnest on the ground – in Hollywood and in real life.

If I knew that entering my middle age would mean an era of power-dressing and exuding effortless authority, I'd be fine with that. I'd love to grow old in the mould of someone like International Monetary Fund boss Christine Lagarde, rocking tailored suits and lecturing poor countries about austerity measures. The problem is that absolutely nothing resembling that picture is going to happen for me.

The entire reason I became a journalist was so I'd never have to iron any work clothes. On the occasions in my life when I have worked in an office setting, I have found the strain of identifying a different respectable outfit to wear on each consecutive day to be an intolerable burden – like an actress scrabbling in a teenager's closet daily for a costume to wear to audition for the role of 'adult'.

I have no clear sense of what my future looks like aesthetically but it probably won't be good. 'Rumpled older man' can be charming and endearing. 'Rumpled older woman' just seems like someone who never got her shit together.

But even if I never learn how to wear clothes properly, I can at least take action on my face. It would have been better, of course, if I'd started looking after my face a decade ago, like they tell you to.

'You get the skin you were born with at 20, the skin you buy at 30, and the skin you deserve at 40' – is that how that extremely annoying saying goes? What bollocks. If anything is medievally anti-feminist, it's the idea that we should read *the texture of someone's epidermis* as a chronicle of past sins.

We might as well go back to measuring skull size to test intelligence.

I had a friend once whose mother had instructed her to laugh as infrequently as possible in order to avoid the subsequent wrinkles. Even when highly entertained, she would attempt to maintain an even expression while her body shook silently with suppressed amusement, like someone having a minor stroke. I found it overwhelmingly depressing (though also something of an exciting challenge, obviously).

I don't know about you, but I'd rather laugh uproariously whenever I choose and deal with the resulting facial effects if I start feeling bad about them.

It is enormously sad that wrinkles are viewed as undesirable, since they speak of objectively positive things: laughter, experience, wisdom. The real problem, though, seems to me to be with a society that views visible signs of ageing as abhorrent – but then *also* sharply criticises people who dare do anything to conceal that ageing. One or the other, people!

I am thinking here of actress Renée Zellweger, who managed to single-handedly dominate the global news conversation for about a week in October 2014 when she stepped out in public wearing her face.

'What has she done to it?' raged the discussion. 'How dare she change her face?' This despite the fact that, as some commentators pointed out, many people had been pretty mean about her old face. This despite the fact, too, that many people hadn't properly looked at her face since *Bridget Jones's Diary*, filmed a full 15 years before she debuted the 'new' face.

There was a lot of talk about how what was *really* bothering people was that they had developed some form of meaningful relationship with Zellweger's old face. Well, sorry for you! Unfortunately, that was an entirely one-way relationship as Renée Zellweger had never so much as clapped eyes on *you* and therefore owed you precisely nothing.

'What we all loved about her was those quirky eyes,' someone suggested to me on Twitter. As far as I can make out, though, Zellweger still *has* eyes. Two of them, sitting in the middle of her face, letting her see things as usual. And if we are seriously suggesting that inner quirkiness can be externally manifested only through eye shape, we are heading down a terribly problematic conversational path: are Chinese eyes 'quirkier' than Caucasian eyes?

What a confusing set of messages! You need a Bletchley Park cryptographer to work out what's going on here. Someone like Zellweger is presumably presented with abundant evidence that if she wants to prolong her vocation she needs to keep looking like a dewy infant. Yet when she takes some proactive measures in this direction to invest in her career longevity – from the perspective of her industry, essentially the equivalent of the rest of us going on an Excel course – she gets pilloried!

Where I part ways with Renée is in her apparent refusal to admit that she'd had any surgical work done, however. Zellweger was reported as having attributed her transformation to the fact that she was 'happy'. I am frequently overwhelmed with contentment, but it has never caused my jaw to extend spontaneously.

This strikes me as the equivalent of those women who sleep over for the first time at their lover's house and wake up at the crack of dawn to cake on make-up and straighten their hair so their partner won't think they went to bed with Charlize Theron and woke up with Aileen Wuornos.

It would have made a more dignified statement if Zellweger had said: 'You know what? I literally had my whole face cut up and rearranged. And I did it for *you*, you ungrateful fuckers.'

Barring this, though, it would be great if we could adopt a policy of 'It's your face, so do whatever you like with it'. Whatever makes you smile when you look in the mirror – even if that's the freakish immobility of your eyebrows. Unless that's a swastika tattoo on your forehead, of course.

21

Look it Up

I **love words.**

This is a pretty meaningless statement in isolation, admittedly, a bit like 'I really can't get enough of emptying my bladder'.

I don't love all words. I hate 'moist', but I'm pretty sure this is a common affliction, and the phrase 'moist towelette' – to refer to those warm slivers of paper you get on airplanes – makes me feel slightly ill.

I despise the (fortunately increasingly uncommon) habit of gendering a word by adding 'ess' to it, such as 'authoress', because it feels like a twee little bed frill – and implies that the default root word should always apply only to a male.

There are a few exceptions, however. I admit that I inexplicably find the word 'murderess' both slightly hilarious and also quite glamorous.

In another case, a friend's grandmother grew up Jewish in an anti-Semitic school in apartheid South Africa, and on one occasion during a school assembly the headmaster demanded that all the Jewish students stand up. She did not and was called to account for it.

'I am not a Jew,' she explained, drawing herself up to her full height. 'I am a *Jewess*.'

There's something about the use of the -ess suffix there that seems poignantly dignified and powerful, like the emotional climax of a Spielberg film, so I'll give that specific instance a free pass too.

For someone who is extremely foul-mouthed, I surprise myself in my distaste for the word 'fart' and almost all its slang equivalents, but particularly 'baff'. I'm not as bad as my sister, though, who once told me in my youth to please stop using 'the t-word'. Toilet.

I get unreasonably annoyed by the phrase 'on so many levels' – as in 'That is wrong on so many levels' – because frequently, unless you are referring to the design of a multi-storey building, there is *obviously only one level*.

Another common phrase that drives me to drink is 'in any way, shape or form'. Almost invariably, you only need one of those. I understand that the effect it's aiming at is emphasis – 'I'm not interested in him in any way, shape or form' – but it's used a lot in contexts where that degree of emphasis is unnecessary. It's just meaningless verbiage because people would rather say four words than one.

Don't get me started on people who say they have 'done a 360' on a particular issue, which by definition means that your position has not shifted one iota. I am also troubled by the hyper-inflation affecting percentages: to say that you support something '100%' now suggests relatively weak approval, since you could be supporting it 150%, 500% or 10 gazillion jillion%.

At the end of the day, which is an additional phrase I despise, I'm in a weak position to be snooty about other people's verbal choices. As you may have noticed, for instance, I play distinctly fast and loose with adverbs generally and more specifically the word 'literally', which I apply entirely metaphorically to everything from 'my head literally exploded' to 'I would literally rather die'. After I have made these absurd statements, I will sometimes insert an extra 'literally' for additional force.

'I literally want to kill myself,' I will say cheerily, contemplating some exceptionally insignificant challenge. 'Literally.'

I used to have a far more hard-line approach to these matters. What changed my mind was working at a dictionary.

You'd think it would be the opposite, right? I certainly did. The main reason why I was so excited to get a job at the Oxford English Dictionary (OED) was because I used to spend my life giving people unsolicited and deeply resented advice on word usage.

I literally could not help myself, and I'm using 'literally' here in the good old-fashioned way.

'Ahem,' I'd say, with the giddy rush of mixed exhilaration and shame that accompanies the performance of any compulsive behaviour, 'I think you'll find that "disinterested" means something quite different from the sense you intend there.'

When I started at the OED I basically saw it as a way to win more arguments of this kind – because who the hell would quibble with a lexicographer on word meaning? (Everyone, it turns out.)

What I had failed to realise, though, was that dictionaries are far less prescriptive than you might think. In fact, they're not really prescriptive at all. They're *descriptive*. They look at the way words are being used out there, in the real world, and then document them. That's why, when you look up 'literally', a good dictionary won't say: 'Only ever use this word if everything around it is exactly true.' It'll tell you that that's one sense in which the word is used and another use is metaphorical.

And neither option is 'wrong' or 'right'. They just *are*. Word meanings constantly shift, and dictionaries record those changes without being all judgy.

This was my first realisation from my desk at the OED. The second was that the same boring fights we have about words today have been playing out, in some cases, for over a century. I have always been vocally opposed to the spelling 'alright' (instead of 'all right') but I experienced a weird discomfort when I came across, in the dictionary archives, a letter that had been written to a British newspaper around 1910 making exactly the same plea.

It turns out that the 'alright' spelling dates back to the late 19th century at least, and it makes perfect sense, fitting the pattern of words like 'altogether' and 'already'. Over 100 years later, twats like me are still on some bizarre crusade for the purity of the 'all right' form. *We need to let it go.*

I was seduced by the romance of the OED project. It is the kind of insane human endeavour you don't see very much of any more, in a world fixated on quick outputs and returns. They have been working on this dictionary since 1857 and there have only been two editions. When I say 'they' worked on it, I mean – initially – a lunatic, as you'll know if you've read Simon Winchester's entertaining account of the origins of the OED, *The Professor and the Madman.* A large part of the first edition of the OED was written by a criminally insane murderer imprisoned in a lunatic asylum. It sort of makes sense.

When I started there in 2010, they had been writing the third edition for a decade and by the time I left we were *nowhere.* I mean, maybe about a third of the way through, tops. While I was there we finished the letter 'R', and then there was a party.

They used to start at A and work their way through to Z. But taking a long, hard look at the first two editions, they realised that all the entries close to the start of the alphabet were noticeably weaker, because the editors were new to the job. So for the third edition, they work on letters near the beginning and end of the alphabet simultaneously.

It was very peaceful at work. Nobody spoke. There was not what you would call a carnival atmosphere. The silence was disturbed only by one particular colleague, who would jump out of her seat and scream when the fire alarm went off at exactly the same time every week. You got used to it, though.

It isn't only the people who work at the OED who have an obsessive relationship with it. Members of the public are encouraged to participate by sending in examples of specific words that they find in texts, particularly when they're quite obscure words.

There's one guy in Australia who has sent thousands and thousands of little cards on to which he has painstakingly glued examples of words he has cut out of newspapers, almost daily. To thank him for his work the OED management asked him if he would like to come and have a tour of the dictionary. He declined on the basis that he was too busy with his cuttings and didn't want to fall behind.

The OED occupies a strange place in the public understanding – as the arbiter of linguistic standards but also a kind of general oracle. Once it's in the dictionary, it must be real. This is why people, and corporations, often lobby to get definitions changed.

McDonald's wanted the definition of 'McJob' – a low-paid, dead-end form of work – changed by the OED. The company said it should be defined instead as 'a job that is stimulating, rewarding … and offers skills that last a lifetime', which is not remotely the impression I have ever received from anyone who has worked at McDonald's. In a noteworthy display of corporate might, McDonald's even managed to get a Conservative MP in Britain to introduce a parliamentary motion condemning the pejorative use of McJob.

They didn't succeed in changing the definition. Politicians come and go. The OED is forever.

The British Potato Council – which raises the comical mental image of a group of irate spuds sitting round a boardroom – complained to the OED about the phrase 'couch potato', which it felt was insulting to potatoes. Presumably this council saw potatoes as dynamic, vibrant vegetables, undeserving of being demeaned as slothful TV addicts. The council picketed outside the OED offices to demand the term be changed to 'couch slouch', which admittedly has the benefit of rhyming.

The potatoes lost. Once a word goes into the dictionary, it never comes out. The OED is the Hotel California of reference works.

You'd be amazed at how many people write to the dictionary with words they have made up. They are always convinced that these coinages urgently warrant being standardised into language.

'Dear OED,' they write. 'I would like to submit the word "edunewsatainment", which I have invented to refer to a media product which is part education, part news, and part entertainment.'

Then we'd have to reply and explain that they would need to submit multiple examples of the word being used in different print sources (and not just your personal WhatsApps) over a period of several years.

I always felt bad because I know how exciting it is to make up a word. I made up the word 'coatigan', to refer to a garment that is somewhere between a coat and a cardigan. Then I googled it and found out that I didn't make it up at all. It was already in common use. I was crushed.

There is a vault of words at the OED: a room packed from roof to ceiling with little filing boxes stuffed with words. Most of these will never find their way into the dictionary.

I wanted to do the best I could for these words. I was their advocate, their bridge between illegitimacy and the big-time. Sometimes I thought of myself as a one-woman X Factor judging panel for words hoping to make it.

'And who do we have here, then?' I'd murmur, plucking a long-forgotten word-slip from the vault.

'Subsexual,' it would whisper back. 'I'm Subsexual.'

'Subsexual, hey?' I'd muse, studying it. 'Saucy little thing, aren't you? And what's *your* story?'

'It's always been my dream,' Subsexual would shrug. 'My friend Hypersexual made it in, and my cousin Asexual, and my aunt-who-used-to-be-my-uncle Transsexual ...'

'Touching journey,' I'd nod. 'But when it comes down to it, Subsexual, do you have the full package? I can't help but feel that you lack *substance*.'

'Please,' Subsexual would whimper, crumpling. 'It's my dream.'

'We've all got a dream, kid,' I'd say, tucking Subsexual away in the Not Heading For The Dictionary Any Time Soon pile. 'And I'm living mine. Literally.'

22

Never Read the Comments

Imagine if people behaved in real life the way they do on the internet? You'd have folk walking down the street ranting like lunatics.

'But what about FARM MURDERS?' they'd yell at total strangers.

People would turn to the person sitting next to them on a bus and say things like: 'Just feeling really over it today,' or show them pictures of their breakfast. In group situations, friends would painstakingly tell each other every single thing they were doing, as they were doing it.

'Brunch with the girls!' they'd parrot repeatedly, forking rosa tomatoes into their mouths. 'Scrambled eggs and potato rosti with my favourite ladies! Drinking cappuccinos in the sun, yum!'

People would think you were mad or at least tedious company. Yet online, this shit is normal. People apparently feel freed up to behave in all sorts of astonishing ways the minute they're in range of a wi-fi signal. It does something to our heads, similar to the way some out-there scientists claim inaudible high-frequency sounds can affect brain activity.

Sometimes I imagine people opening up their laptops, cracking their knuckles and saying: 'Let's see what kinds of crazy provocation I, as an otherwise perfectly normal individual, can stir up on the internet today!'

It's a bit like everyone's drunk, all the time, online. Oversharing with strangers, picking fights, getting needlessly emotional over tiny things. The internet is like the perpetual closing time at the biggest bar in the world.

I'm no different, of course. There is a vast – and growing – chasm between my online persona and my real-life personality. Online, I am braver, chattier and about a million times more confrontational than offline. In the real world, I will go to absurd lengths to avoid confrontation, silently accepting the entirely wrong food order in a restaurant, for instance. On the internet, I'm out there like a torch-wielding dogmatist, baying for blood. Come at me, world!

People talk a lot about this liberating effect being attributable to the 'anonymity' of the internet, but a lot of us aren't anonymous at all online. Almost everything I do on the interwebs is under my real name, accompanied by a fraudulently flattering photograph.

The one exception, which is perhaps telling, is my TripAdvisor account. I write those reviews under the cloak of a pseudonym, clearly because I fear on some level that if I say something negative, I will be gunned down on the street by a hotel manager who moonlights as an assassin.

And it's *always* something negative, though truthful, because I never bother writing reviews for the nice places. I get absurdly thrilled by TripAdvisor's emails to me, sycophantically informing me what a splendid job I'm doing.

'Did you realise how many travellers you've guided with your advice?' the last email read. 207! I actually punched the air with excitement. Now 207 people know that the Belvedere Estate has a major shongololo problem!

(It's not called the Belvedere Estate, obviously. As if I'd risk my life like that!)

When I'm not skulking around TripAdvisor in disguise, though, I'm surfing the web as myself. Just a slightly different version. There are days when I have to cling consciously to my last scraps of decorum online. My Twitter drafts folder – tweets composed and then thankfully set aside before sending – could be submitted to the South African Human Rights Commission in one shameful dossier.

I am intrigued, however, by the people for whom there is no online brake whatsoever. There are Twitter users whose timelines constitute an endless stream of abuse, sent forth almost indiscriminately to real-life humans. And there are those who go out of their way to leave comments of extraordinary vitriol on relatively insignificant online news articles. These people are usually anonymous.

I have stopped reading the online comments on articles I write – particularly on op-ed pieces. This makes me quite sad because sometimes people say really nice things, which make me feel proud and happy. Sometimes they also say pretty useful things: constructive feedback, factual corrections, interesting additions to the debate. But so often the comments are so genuinely hateful that I have had to wean myself off the habit of reading them.

When journalists whose work is posted online tell people this, they often accuse you of arrogance – of not wanting to engage with readers or of thinking you're too good to listen to advice.

Then I say: 'Imagine, if you will, that someone bursts into your workplace, where you're sitting trying to do the best job that you can, overworked and underpaid. This person then whips down their pants and proceeds to piss all over your desk, while hurling abuse about your appearance and character.'

Would you simply accept this as part of your job? Would you say: 'Oh well, it's only two out of every ten people who burst in here who urinate over my stationery and shout terrible personal insults at me. The other eight are pretty level-headed.'

As much as I try to convince myself that the worst commenters are using one hand to pound their tiny genitals while the other bashes out their hate-filled words, the problem is that their bile tends to stay with you.

'Rebecca is a rug-munching cunt with a wasted Oxford education,' is one that I'll probably need deep hypnosis to remove from my memory.

I once wrote an article criticising sexist billboards erected by a local strip club, Mavericks, which attracted hundreds of memorable comments.

'Rebecca comes across as a neurotic sex-negative house wife,' one began. 'Ironically she will most likely marry a man who will visit strip clubs.' Spooky! *How do you know my future, Gypsy Rose?*

Someone else wrote: 'I bet this Rebecca tool works at Mavericks, auditioned for these ads and was horribly turned down, now the jealousy of not being on one of those billboards drove her to post this.' But how can I be *both* a neurotic sex-negative housewife and a stripper?

'Rebecca must have the painters in,' wrote another, which is a hilarious and original reference to the female menses. It's apparently widely believed that the arrival of one's menstrual cycle induces a sudden uncharacteristic disdain for sexist billboards.

'Written by a hormonal woman ... it shows,' said another. And more, apparently reading from the same page of Awesome Bro Comebacks: 'This piece was definitely spurred on by a certain monthly visitor.'

'Rebecca obviously has sand in her vagina,' wrote another. (I think this would have been more effective if he had added: 'Cos she's a beach.')

'Don't you have dishes to do?'

'Poor Rebeccy is just worked up 'cause she isn't half way as hot as the girls in these posters.'

'Work on your body, relationship and sexuality then your man would not feel the need to go to Mavericks.'

'Shame ... Rebecca's man cheated on her with a stripper.'

'Rebecca, why aren't you in the kitchen?'

'Soz but Reb ain't eye candy. That's the real problem here.'

I find it hard to accept that online writers should simply stomach this puerile rudeness as part of their job. I wouldn't be allowed to walk into a stranger's workplace and yell: 'WHY HAVE YOU GOT YOUR TITS IN A TANGLE YOU FREAKY HO?', so I don't see why they should feel entitled to do the same to me.

One answer, of course, is to employ moderators who continually scan comments for slanderous invective. I spent a month working at the *Guardian* in the UK, where they have a full-time team of moderators doing just that. I think it must be a terrible job, to be exposed to so much nastiness, day in, day out.

Forcing people to log in to comment using their real social media profiles apparently helps a bit – although not that much, as you'd know if you've ever visited the diabolical hellhole that is News24 comments. There, people are apparently perfectly agreeable to using their personal Facebook accounts to spew racial hate speech.

A number of prestigious international media outlets have banned online comments altogether. In September 2013, *Popular Science* announced that it was shutting off online comments on the grounds that research has shown comments can influence people's perception of the content of the article. The fact that comments can influence how people view the article's content is fine if the article consists of me ranting about sexist billboards. It's less fine if you're writing about some major climate change research, for instance, and a slew of uncivil comments lead other readers to doubt the reliability of a proven scientific discovery. It does seem amazing that a bunch of people shouting 'BUT CLIMATE CHANGE CAN'T EXIST COS THERE ARE STILL TREES' could cause others to reconsider the issue – but apparently most of us are more simple than we think.

In 2014, American writer Kathleen Hale became so fixated with an online commenter who left a negative review of her book on a website that she actually tracked down the writer and confronted her. Hale was widely condemned for this, since the reviewer had done nothing more than express a critical opinion.

I have to admit that part of me deeply empathised with Hale. I recently became quite fixated with uncovering the true identity of one particular denizen of the internet: an individual who continuously tweeted homophobic, sexist, racist abuse at me and many other people. Though his Twitter handle was a normal first name and last name, the fact that I could find no other information about this person online led me to believe that it was a pseudonym.

Reader, I went so far as to discuss the matter with a private investigator who specialises in digital research. That is how obsessed I became. What led me to put the brakes on the project was a simple question posed by my online PI: 'What do you hope to achieve from this?'

If I lived somewhere like the UK I would have answered that question with: 'Reporting him to the police.' In England, a number of people have gone to jail for abusive tweets. I can well imagine how the average overworked South African police detective would take it if you arrived at the station, pushed to the front of the queue past rape survivors and hijack victims, and announced that you wished them to investigate someone being horrible to you on Twitter.

What I hoped to achieve, in all honesty, was an elaborate revenge daydream. I saw myself establishing that my internet foe was some weak little nerd who worked at an office. Then I saw myself arriving at his office door to confront him – *after* I had delivered his boss a folder containing printouts of his online hate speech.

The more I thought about it, though, the more insane the plan seemed. And dangerous. While researching him, I discovered that the dude in question had previously boasted of being a Special Forces Operator for the South African military, and of working as a mercenary in Iraq. I suspected he was lying but it didn't really seem like a hunch worth risking my life for. Reluctantly, I let it go. I blocked him on Twitter and tried to forget he existed, pouring his hate into the universe on a daily basis.

Besides some of those hotel managers on TripAdvisor probably feel exactly the same way about me.

23

Don't Call Us, We Won't Call You

Alexander Graham Bell's first phone call consisted of the words: 'Mr Watson, come here, I want to see you.'

If he'd known it would go down in history he would surely have put a little more work into it. I mean, that sounds like the first line of a soft-porn Sherlock Holmes adaptation. Neil Armstrong apparently spent hours thinking about what he was going to radio down to Houston from the Moon. His brother even claimed he wrote his 'One small step' line well in advance of his trip.

And thank goodness Armstrong was so acutely alive to the burden of the historical moment! Imagine the anticlimax if he'd said something like 'Hi, it's me. Just arrived. Turns out there's nothing here.'

Having said that, when people are asked to test the sound quality on a microphone, it seems they suddenly lose all powers of speech beyond

'Testing, testing,' or 'Hello.' Maybe Graham Bell suffered the same kind of stage fright. Obviously what he *really* wanted to say was something along the lines of 'Holy shit, can you believe I'm talking to you and you're not in the same room?' Or perhaps: 'This is *way* better than two cans joined by a piece of string!'

That first phone call was more than 130 years ago and since then the sense of elation that accompanied telephonic communication has dwindled for many of us.

I have a pathological dread of both making and receiving phone calls that appears to be intensifying as I age. After lengthy thought, I have identified the three major reasons why.

Firstly, phone calls constitute the most direct invasion of someone's space outside of actual physical contact. It strikes me that there is something downright arrogant about expecting someone to drop literally everything they are doing at a specific moment in order to attend to your voice, particularly if it is an unsolicited call that is not conveying a life-threatening emergency.

Secondly, I find it much, much harder to say no to something over the phone than in text. Being put on the spot often forces you into rash, snap decisions about things in order to avoid awkwardness. 'Write a 10 000 word piece by 9am tomorrow about cat people vs dog people? For free? Um, sure! Why not? Perfect!'

My normal approach is to agree enthusiastically to absolutely everything someone suggests to me over the phone and then immediately rescind it over email, which I imagine is quite frustrating for everyone involved.

Thirdly, it is often extremely difficult to contain the length of a phone call without being pretty forceful or downright rude, neither of which I excel at verbally. You can try that thing where you make garbled sounds into the phone and pretend that your reception is breaking up, but it's a transparent little ruse. If you're a business person you can always say, 'I'm just going into a meeting.' But as someone with slim prospects of ever being invited to a meeting that line would be an obvious lie.

I know that I'm not alone in these views because I once expressed them on Twitter and received a torrent of vigorous agreement. In fact, it appeared that almost nobody was willing to stand up and be counted as a phone call advocate.

Perhaps that's because people whose jobs require them to make a lot of calls – salespeople, estate agents, PR people and, um, journalists – capitalise off precisely what I've outlined above: catching you on the back foot. They feed off the vulnerability that accompanies that space.

Where possible – and I accept that this is a luxury granted only to people who benefit from advanced communications infrastructure – there are plenty of sensible reasons for preferring email or text-based contact to phone calls.

Primary among them is that by corresponding in writing you have a concrete record of exactly what has been said and agreed to. This is also terrifying. Ever since the Pistorius trial, I have tried to make my WhatsApp messages to my girlfriend especially loving in case they are ever read in open court to support the idea that I murdered her.

This tangible record is also what screwed over the world's diplomats in the Wikileaks scandal – though if that's the stuff that they were happy to put down in writing, I dread to think what they're murmuring to each other over the phone. To learn that the globe's top diplomats communicate like mean girls passing notes in maths class was knowledge I could have done without, however much it led me to consider that I might be ideally suited for an ambassadorial post.

Some people argue that it is much easier to misread someone's tone over emails than during phone calls, leading to unnecessary drama. This is true. Sometimes when I receive an email that I can't quite interpret, I like to read it out loud in varying tones – sulky aggression, followed by bright cheeriness – to see which rings true. But this problem is what emoticons and emojis were invented to counter.

Purists see emoticons as a mark of immaturity. They have a genuinely useful purpose, however, because misinterpretation is a perpetual feature of human communication. As far back as 1887, writer Ambrose Bierce proposed something similar to the modern-day smiley, 'to be appended, with the full stop, to every jocular or ironical sentence'.

When people overuse emoticons it is undeniably irritating, like being attacked by a troupe of bipolar clowns. As writer Anne Trubek pointed out in a piece on the history of emoticons, this is something that has happened throughout history whenever new typographical features were introduced.

One of the first punctuation marks was a space – because, incredibly, people used to write without any spaces between words. Fools! Then some genius figured out that the tricky business of reading would be a shitload easier if the words were separated. Other punctuation marks followed to facilitate reading aloud.

Trubek records that during the Middle Ages scribes were so excited about these thrilling new features of written language – the humble comma, the unremarkable question mark – that they used to just vomit them all over the page. The more,,,, the merrier!!!!! But then we calmed down, and it's to be hoped that the same is happening with emoticons for people over the age of 16.

So I'm not at all averse to a sensibly placed emoticon, particularly when I'm corresponding with someone I don't know very well. Anyway, it isn't only email that lends itself to tonal ambiguity. It is also possible to misinterpret someone's tone when they're speaking to you, especially if you can't see the person's face.

There used to be all sorts of etiquette suggestions about how best to carry out a phone call back in the day when the technology was still new. Even then, it seems that phone calls often brought out the worst in people. In 1910 the Bell Telephone franchise put out adverts warning against 'Dr. Jekyll and Mr Hyde at the telephone'.

'Courteous and considerate co-operation is as essential at the telephone as in the office or home,' they sternly admonished, reminding users that both parties were 'anxious and probably impatient'.

Early phone companies were also adamant that the most unforgiveable sin of telephone conduct was to begin your conversation with 'hello'.

'Would you rush into an office or up to the door of a residence and blurt out "Hello! Hello! Who am I talking to?"' lectured AT&T.

They proposed instead that one should start a phone call with: 'Mr Wood, of Curtis and Sons, wishes to talk with Mr White.' Imagine what a gigantic wanker you'd seem if you did that today!

There is something to be said for people immediately identifying themselves on the phone, though. I get chills thinking of phone conversations where I have no idea who the other party is, who is nonetheless chatting away in a manner that suggests breezy familiarity. If you don't ask who they are right at the beginning, you're fucked. Then you have to restrict your conversation to vague generalities like 'How's ... life?' in the hope that they will eventually say something concrete enough to pin them down.

There ought to be a special place in hell reserved for people who leave voicemail messages, too, because who has the time to listen to those? I used to until I realised that every second message was from my technologically un-savvy mother saying: 'Hello? Hello? Rebecca, are you there? You just said something, so why are you being quiet now?'

The one aspect of telephonic conduct that my mother has really mastered, however, is how to deal with obscene phone calls. She keeps a small police-regulation whistle within reach of the phone at all times. At one stage during my adolescence, her eagerness to bring out the whistle was such that in *any* ambiguous telephonic situation (such as, say, a stranded daughter phoning tearily from a crackly call-box) she would grab the whistle with unseemly glee and blast it down the line like a Bafana Bafana supporter with a vuvuzela after a goal.

'Such filth,' she would say afterwards, snapping the phone back on to its cradle.

Do obscene phone calls still happen? I feel that the advent of cellphones has, counter-intuitively, made them less common. A few years ago I did get a series of phone calls from a man energetically masturbating while a porn flick played in the background.

You may be confused by the words 'a series of' in that sentence, but the truth is that I couldn't stop myself answering the phone. I was spurred by the same motivation that kept people watching *Lost*: that deep-seated belief in the possibility that it's about to get more interesting.

But the main reason I kept on answering and listening intently was that I was struck by the possibility that I might be able to pick up a clue as to his identity or geographical position from the ambient sounds of the call. Something like a specific and highly localised form of birdsong in the background, which would enable me to whack my thigh and cry, 'By gum, the Knysna Loerie! You're nabbed, son!'

Then I remembered that I couldn't tell a birdsong from a police siren, so I gave up and let him reach his shuddering climax to the sexy purr of 'The caller you have dialled is not available'.

The very existence of obscene phone calls represents another victory for email over phone, since pornographic content generally gets smoothly redirected to your email's spam folder. I admit I much prefer my spam folder to my actual inbox because everyone in it is so friendly and so understanding about my erectile dysfunction. I also greatly enjoy the habit among scammers of addressing me with the words 'Dearly beloved', as if you're the only two mourners in attendance at a tiny funeral.

If there is a funeral to be had, I wish it could be for the phone call. If I had the guts, when people asked for my number, I'd say: 'I'm afraid my phone is for emergencies only and for ordering pizza. But here's my email address – mail me any time.' Until copious amounts of therapy grants me this courage, I'll be anxiously ignoring your call. :)

24

When Losing is Winning

On my very first day at the University of Oxford, I was having a beer with my friend Konstantin at a local watering hole. Konstantin and I were in the same boat: a rickety little rowboat from the colonies. We were both South African, had both won scholarships to Oxford, and were now dealing with the terrifying reality of actually being there.

'Do you speak Boer?' a posh English student had asked me earlier that day, upon hearing where I was from. That was his second question. His opening gambit was: 'Sub-equatorial habitation! Who'd have thought it possible?'

The scholarship application process that had led me to this point was among the most daunting things I'd ever encountered. There were multiple rounds of interviews, all carried out by panels of judges with inscrutable poker faces and CVs longer than the iTunes terms and conditions. Their questions were hard and scary. My major objective was to get through them without having to fake a Victorian swoon and run out of the room.

'What is the worst thing that you think people say about you behind your back?' one judge asked me. I froze.

Obviously there was no chance of replying with anything approximating the truth, which was: 'That I drink too much and have a slovenly disregard for my personal appearance.'

'That I'm ... too private,' I said weakly. *Lies!* The only way it could have been a more transparent lie is if I had responded: 'That I spend too much time on charity work.'

Despite these falsehoods, I was on a pretty good wicket until the finals of one particular scholarship. Finalists were accommodated at by far the poshest place I'd ever stayed, a boutique guest house in Johannesburg. The night before the interview, we had dinner with the judges: august representatives of South African academia, judiciary and business.

It was basically the most stressful speed-dating session ever because you had to move from judge to judge, purring nuggets of erudition into their ears.

When there is a million-rand education at stake, there is no prospect of conversation ever taking place in a sincere and relaxed fashion. It must be hell for the judges. Everyone competes to present themselves in the most intelligent, bewitching way possible. In this respect I suppose it is not unlike actual speed-dating, except that your chances of ending up in someone's bed after 14 Jägermeisters are substantially lower.

My interview the following day did not go well. This happened around a decade ago and it is no exaggeration to say that eight years later I was still waking up in a cold sweat from nightmares about it.

I partially blame my friend Matt, who had won one of these scholarships and told me that the key to success was simply admitting when you didn't know the answer to something. His advice was solid; my application of it was not. Admitting ignorance is fine when it's a technical question in a sphere far removed from your own: a philosophy student being asked to recite pi to 100 decimal places, for instance. It is less fine when the question is something you should reasonably be expected to have an opinion on as an engaged South African.

I simply took Matt's advice too far.

'What do you think is the future of the Tripartite Alliance?' they asked me.

'I don't know,' I said confidently.

They stared at me. One judge, who I got the sense had been sort of marginally rooting for me up to that point, tried to hint that this wasn't an optional question.

'You must have *some* opinion,' she prodded gently. 'Do you think a split could be in the offing?'

I did not, in fact, have some opinion. They might as well have asked me my views on string theory. At that stage of my life I read the *Mail & Guardian* but not every week, and I tended to skip past the boring bits at the front.

'I just don't think I'm qualified to answer that,' I said falteringly.

In the silence that followed, I knew all was lost.

A few years later, on a trip to Greece, I had a flashback to that moment. Greece is a traumatic place to visit for anyone continually afraid of being unmasked as mentally feeble because even their street graffiti is not 'Jou ma se poes' so much as quotations from the *Iliad*. Anyway, I was having a bikini wax and in the course of desultory conversation my wax technician inquired what I studied.

'Linguistics,' I replied.

'Oh,' she said, ripping hair from my nether regions. 'What do you think of the potential existence of a Proto-Indo-European language?'

I didn't win the respect of that woman and I didn't win one of those fancy scholarships, as you've probably guessed. If I had, this book would be an authoritative guide to the Tripartite Alliance, rather than a loose collection of anecdotes.

But I did get to Oxford, on a less fancy scholarship. And being there felt a lot like being in those scholarship interviews, every single day.

There Konstantin and I were, sipping our beer and talking about how weird Oxford was. Konstantin had won a prestigious scholarship because he could give you the kind of insights into the Tripartite Alliance that would turn you into a political analyst overnight. We'd both applied for the same college – a res, in South African terms – on the grounds that it had a reputation for being the least stuffy and most left wing.

To put this into perspective, what this meant was that our croquet quad was named after Ho Chi Minh.

Every 'bop' – a disco, essentially – also ended with the playing of the 1984 song 'Free Nelson Mandela', by The Specials. We never had the heart to tell them that Mandela's liberation had already been taken care of because everyone sang along so lustily.

We were having that beer on our first day and a man who was clearly homeless, as well as toothless, sidled over and perched on the end of our bench. He bummed a cigarette and, like that evil Greek bikini-waxer, asked me what I was studying.

'Linguistics,' I replied.

He nodded, knowledgeably.

'Know any Finnish, do you?' he asked. 'No,' I replied, rolling my eyes. *Get away from me, loon-man! I have a fascinating conversation to conclude on how kak the Brits are!*

'Interesting language, Finnish,' he said, burping. 'Highly agglutinative.' This was the preamble to a lecture on the *complex morphology of Finnish*.

When he eventually took his departure – probably to finish writing a seminal linguistics monograph in a ditch – I turned to Konstantin in horror.

'You realise what this means?' I hissed. 'In Oxford, even homeless people know more about my area of study than I do!'

This terrifying initial realisation turned out to be pretty much spot-on.

There was a porter at another Oxford college – a man tasked with sorting post and handing out keys – who had a doctorate in linguistics. From Oxford.

Our phonetics classes turned out to be particularly surreal. Phonetics is the study of speech sounds. It's what the character of Henry Higgins, from *My Fair Lady*, specialises in. Henry Higgins could hear a stranger speak three words and would immediately be able to tell him what road he grew up on. I desperately wanted to acquire this superpower for myself.

In our second lesson, our professor walked in with an unknown man. The professor explained what would happen next, while I pinched myself to check that I wasn't dreaming. For every lesson for the rest of the term, this man would come to class and simply speak at us in his mother tongue. Our job was to listen and phonetically transcribe what he was saying. At the end of term, we would be required to tell the professor what language the man was speaking. He hastened to assure us that it was not a language that anybody in our extremely international class would be familiar with.

I used the rest of the term to practise my Garfield doodle and pass notes to my friend Cristina. Since I hadn't a hope in hell of guessing the language, my only option was racial profiling of the speaker.

'He looks a bit Chinese,' I would write to Cristina. 'Do you think it might be Chinese????'

'Can't be, dude!' she would reply. 'May [a fellow student] is Chinese!'

Cristina ended up almost getting it right. She guessed that it was a form of Cambodian because she'd had an ex-boyfriend who'd fled the Khmer Rouge as a child. It turned out to be an obscure Vietnamese dialect.

Despite my evident lack of ability in the field of phonetics, after graduating from Oxford I was called for a job interview at the BBC, to be a pronunciation linguist.

Until I saw the job description I had no idea that such a career existed. But it turns out that major broadcasters need to have someone on site to tell newsreaders how to pronounce difficult words. Words such as the name of the Icelandic volcano, Eyjafjallajökull – that's ay-uh-fyat-luh-yoe-kuutl – which looks like a cat just walked across your keyboard. The 2010 World Cup was approaching and they knew there would be a whole bunch of footballers with exotic names.

You almost never see a job advert that requires a postgraduate degree in linguistics, so I felt like I *had* to apply for it. To call my application a 'pack of lies' would be overstating it a bit, but I did make the claim that I had a 'good working knowledge of the International Phonetic Alphabet'. This wasn't true. I could undertake very basic phonetic transcription of English, but that's where it ended.

I was interviewed in a cell-like room at BBC headquarters by two intimidatingly glamorous pronunciation linguists. After some soft general inquiries, one said: 'You'll be taking a test after this interview, but we've just got some really fun, intriguing little exercises for you to do in front us right now.'

And she pushed a piece of paper across the table.

They had provided me with a list of words written in the International Phonetic Alphabet with a cryptic squiggle in the middle of each one. They were symbols I had never seen before. In retrospect, I think they might have been guttural sounds in languages from the Indian subcontinent. At the time, it was like coming face to face with the Rosetta Stone.

'Can you just pronounce each one in turn for us, please,' she said.

If this happened to me today, I like to think that I would have the necessary sense simply to remove myself from the situation. I'd say: 'I'm terribly sorry, but there seems to have been some sort of ludicrous mistake. I thought this was an interview to be a weather girl.'

Instead, I picked up the list and inspected it. I gave a little sigh, as if to say, 'Don't insult me with this trifling task.' And then I started working my way down the list. For each word, I produced a strained, unplaceable gurgle, very softly.

'Eeeeewwwwwggggrrrr,' I murmured. 'Ahhhhhhhyyyyyyyyxx.'

They said nothing, but took copious notes. The notes probably said 'DUMBASS DUMBASS WHO IS THIS BIG FAKING DUMBO', interspersed with Garfield doodles. It was testament to their restraint that they did not start making neck-slashing gestures at each other. Perhaps they simply couldn't believe what an amazing story this would make for office drinks later.

The next question required me to transcribe vowels in French and Afrikaans, two languages I had claimed fluency in on my application. (Clearly in my head I was applying for a job at the SABC, where it is not uncommon for applicants to weave magnificent untruths into their CVs.) My hand shook so violently that I couldn't even get the pencil to stay on the page. It vibrated like the needle on a lie detector. I think this was the point at which they started feeling genuinely sorry for me because they began to say 'You can leave that one out, if you like', and other similar things.

There was more, a lot more, but even the strain of recalling it has caused my T-shirt to soak through with sweat. After a seeming eternity they released me to carry out a phonetics exam in a separate room. I was given transcriptions of 12 different languages and told to identify them. They looked a bit Slavic.

'Hungarian,' I wrote under one.

Then I stopped. *Is Hungarian actually a language?* I wondered. *Is that like claiming they speak 'Namibian' in Namibia?*

How is it possible that I am at a BBC interview to be a pronunciation linguist if I do not know whether Hungarian is a language?

I didn't get that job.

You win some, you lose some. At Oxford I lost, mainly. But the ultimate result of my series of losses was a net gain. There will always be people who are cleverer, more talented and harder-working than you are. People who know whether Hungarian is a real language and can whip you up a mean goulash on the side.

There's a real sense of liberation in that realisation. Take pride in what you do know and Google what you don't. The Tripartite Alliance is on its last legs, by the way.

25

Love Thy Neighbour

Should you make friends with your neighbours?
There are differing opinions on this matter from various influential cultural sources. The Bible says yes, obviously. 'Love thy neighbour as thyself,' though this is open to interpretation if you're prone to self-hatred.

The old proverb 'Good fences make good neighbours' suggests a more ambiguous sentiment: that amicable neighbourly relations can best be maintained when there are clear boundaries.

The apartheid government used to describe its policy of racial segregation as 'good neighbourliness', which gives the phrase an enduring, creepy ring.

And then there's the Australian soapie *Neighbours*, which is basically a paean to how awesome it is to get all up in each other's business. 'Neighbours,' runs its theme tune, 'should be there for one another/That's when good neighbours become good friends.'

I remain deeply conflicted about whether befriending your neighbours is a good idea. I feel a bit guilty expressing this because at the time of writing I have lovely neighbours. But it's rare to hit the sweet spot: sufficient cordiality to turn to them in time of need (say, being chased by an intruder with a hunting knife), but enough distance not to feel you have to fill them in on your emotional status every time you bump into them on the stairs.

Once you befriend your neighbours, it makes it more difficult to complain about stuff they do. My girlfriend and I once experienced a situation whereby our upstairs neighbour, with whom we had no relationship, clomped overhead with high heels on at 3am almost every night. It might seem like a small thing but at the time it utterly consumed us.

We simply didn't understand why she couldn't take her high heels *off*. Was she trampling her own grapes for wine? Isn't it nice to hang loose when you get home? I rip my clothes off the minute I have one foot through the door, like a chimp safely back in its enclosure after being made to dance for tourists in a top hat and tails.

Every night we would send her a frostily polite text message. The same one, saved as a template. 'Hi, would you mind taking off your shoes? We have to be up early in the morning and the noise prevents us from sleeping.'

Then the clop-clop would continue for about ten minutes, and suddenly, pointedly, stop. It was torture, night after night. We could talk of little else.

'This is what body corporates are for,' friends exhorted. 'Approach the body corporate.'

And so we did. The chair of the body corporate proposed a mediation session in neutral territory, at the chair's flat.

I couldn't think of anything worse. To be brought face to face with our cloven-hoofed nemesis and have to talk it out like adults. Besides, I couldn't understand what there was to talk out. *Why couldn't she just take off her fucking shoes?*

The day approached. I insisted on carrying out role-plays with Jeanine. 'I'll be you, and you be her,' I'd say. I had no intention of doing any of the confrontational work myself. 'We'll do good cop, bad cop,' I said. 'I'll be nice and you be horrible.'

We trudged upstairs like prisoners en route to the gallows, sweaty and clutching a bottle of wine. I had no idea if this was appropriate or not, since it seemed to lend an air of unlikely jollity to proceedings, but I thought our tongues might be emboldened by a few glasses of Sauvignon Blanc.

We entered. Our nemesis was already there, seated stiffly. We exchanged icy greetings. She declined a glass of wine. We did not.

Nobody seemed ready to bring up the purpose of the gathering, so we made small talk. The weather. The flat block. The municipality.

We sipped our wine.

And then something unexpected happened. Utterly without meaning to, we slipped into an entirely engrossing conversation. Politics, news, the state of contemporary South Africa. Our nemesis turned out to share comfortingly similar views on current issues. She was an intelligent, well-read, lively conversationalist.

We loved her.

We'd deliberately arranged a social event just over an hour later, to give us a guaranteed out. I checked the time and realised, to my horror, that we had to depart in five minutes.

'Um,' I said, awkwardly. 'I'm afraid we have to leave just now.' Not one word about shoes of any kind had been exchanged.

The body corporate chair took control. 'About why we're here,' she said.

Our new best friend turned to us. 'I can't always promise to take my shoes off,' she said kindly. 'What I can advise you to do is visit a trained audiologist and have specialist earplugs fitted.'

Bad cop nodded enthusiastically. 'We definitely will!' she said happily. 'And if *we're* ever making too much noise, you just let us know!'

It was the worst possible outcome, but we'd only realise that the next day, when the wine wore off. At the time, we trotted out exultantly. 'She is *so nice*,' Jeanine said.

'We must *definitely* have her over,' I agreed.

We've never felt able to complain since.

Despite this fiasco, Jeanine retains a heartfelt belief in the importance of establishing friendly relations with neighbours.

'Two words,' she says darkly, whenever I beg to differ. 'Kitty Genovese.'

Kitty Genovese was a woman in New York who was stabbed to death near her home in 1964. What made the incident something of a case study was that a reported 38 people heard or observed the attack, and did nothing to stop it. (The figure was later amended down to a mere 12 people, but try telling my girlfriend that.)

The term 'Genovese syndrome', also known as the 'bystander effect', was subsequently coined to refer to the phenomenon where people don't offer any help to a victim in need. The incident is also taken as emblematic of the alienation of urban life, which is sort of what Jeanine's getting at. If Kitty had occasionally asked her neighbours over for a Windhoek and a bowl of Dorito's, wouldn't they have felt more compelled to act?

I do see where she's coming from. I like the *idea* of being part of a neighbourly community, as much as that very word – community – strikes me as utterly alien.

My friend Kim had a job interview recently in which she was asked what role she played in her community. Huh? I would have gazed at them in dopey confusion. What community, exactly?

Maybe they wouldn't have asked her that if she were white. When journalists write about black people in South Africa, we often mention their 'community'.

'Community members took to the streets in a service-delivery protest,' we'll write. 'Tensions have been simmering in this community for some time.'

It's almost always reserved for black people, though, because – I dunno, Ubuntu and 'it takes a village', and stuff. Whites live in 'neighbourhoods', blacks live in 'communities'.

It's bullshit, obviously, but I'm afraid in South Africa it's a cast-iron journalistic rule. Just like the regulation compelling us to describe townships as either 'sprawling' or 'ramshackle', Julius Malema as a 'firebrand', and comedian Jim Carrey as a 'rubber-faced funny-man'. Them's the rules.

I have no sense of belonging to a community. Gays are often *assumed* to have a community, but I'm not clear exactly what form it's supposed to take. I have gay friends but that doesn't seem quite sufficient. If we were a community, wouldn't we get together and sing or something? I do like a karaoke evening once in a while, but I'm not sure that cuts the mustard.

I believe a lot of people get their sense of community from church, but that's out of the question for me. People who cycle always seem to be really into each other, though it makes my bum sore.

If I lived in the suburbs, I could join a neighbourhood watch. Nothing brings middle-class South Africans together like the threat of crime.

I have a friend whose neighbourhood watch, in Cape Town's northern suburbs, even has its own WhatsApp group. Now *that's* a community. On it, members issue coded warnings about unexpected arrivals on their pristine streets. 'Two Bravos on Rosetree Lane,' they'll say. A Bravo is a black person. 'Unidentified Charlie outside Woolworths.' A Charlie is a coloured person.

As a Best White, I like to think I wouldn't get on well in that community. But who knows? Maybe after a few years of assiduously chlorinating my swimming pool I'd just assimilate to their racist norms and spend my evenings glued to the window for some Bravo-spotting.

Still, I think I'd rather do without that particular form of community. I'll stick to smiling falsely at my neighbours on the stairs and bank on that being enough to secure a 10111 call if the screaming starts.

26

Understanding Betrayal

One of the many reasons why I'm probably not cut out for a career in journalism, despite it being my chosen vocation, is that after talking to people I almost always find them less awful than I'd imagined.

I once interviewed a convicted prisoner who'd scored highly in his matric exams. He had soulful brown eyes and a pleasant, gentle manner. I was charmed by him. At the end of our conversation I asked, almost in passing, what he was in jail for.

'Rape,' he said evenly. I almost dropped my notebook in horror.

I like to think that I wouldn't come face to face with someone like Prime Evil – apartheid death squad commander Eugene de Kock – and walk away feeling a bit sorry for him. But I just can't be sure.

I recently read Jacob Dlamini's *Askari*, which devotes quite a lot of space to De Kock's death squad, and was struck by the detail that De Kock shared his anti-anxiety medication with a black struggle activist who was recruited to betray his comrades.

It's not that I find the fact that De Kock shared his meds endearing. I don't. But the idea that De Kock had to take anxiety medication for panic attacks makes him slightly more human.

The problem is that very few people are cartoonishly evil in the way that you've pictured.

I was reminded of this in 2013 when Adrian Leftwich died. Leftwich was a member of an anti-apartheid organisation called the African Resistance Movement (ARM). The now almost-forgotten ARM carried out works of sabotage against South African infrastructure, rather than people. They blew up electricity pylons and railway cables – the kind of acts of sabotage that carried a minimum mandatory sentence of five years, but anything up to the death sentence.

Leftwich was arrested in July 1964 after police searched his Cape Town flat and found a training document schooling the reader in the use of explosives.

He was taken into solitary confinement and beaten, he said later. 'But it was nothing, absolutely nothing, in comparison to what other people in South Africa and elsewhere have been subjected to at the hands of political police,' he wrote, in a 2002 essay called 'I Gave the Names'.

In exchange for his own freedom, Leftwich betrayed his friends and colleagues. In some cases, he testified at their trials. All of them, bar one, went to prison. Some to Robben Island.

Leftwich was 24 years old. He had previously written passionately about the importance of sacrifice and commitment to the struggle. The judge at one of the trials at which Leftwich testified said that to refer to Leftwich as a rat would be unfair to rats.

Leftwich fled overseas. Reading 'I Gave the Names', I felt sorry for him.

'For about fifteen years I lived as if I were half-awake, half-dead,' he wrote. He married and divorced twice in quick succession. He developed a dependency on sleeping pills and was haunted by nightmares of the security police.

But he was alive, and free, which was a luxury not granted to many of his anti-apartheid comrades.

I felt sorry for him because I wondered what I would have done in the same position, at age 24. We all like to think that we would be the ones who'd hold out.

Younger white South Africans like me love to think that we'd have been among that select number opposing apartheid from the frontlines, and then not betraying our comrades when the security police came calling.

But would we have been?

Dlamini's *Askari* tells the story of black South Africans captured by the apartheid police and confronted with the choice of betrayal, torture or death. Some chose betrayal, though it wasn't a real 'choice'. It wasn't that they believed in apartheid ideology. It was that they wanted to live and wanted their families to live.

Others did not crack under torture. They refused to denounce the ANC and were killed.

Those who 'turned', Dlamini writes, were clearly haunted by their actions. Many of them surrendered to drink or drugs. What value is a life, if living is tolerable only when you're rendered sufficiently oblivious to forget – for a moment – your own shame?

Adrian Leftwich tried to make peace with the comrades he betrayed. Some accepted his olive branch; others did not.

'I Gave the Names' is haunting. It's impossible to read it without confronting questions about yourself. Questions about courage, absolution and forgiveness.

I wrote an article about Leftwich in 2013, when he died after succumbing to lung cancer. At the time, he was a respected academic at the University of York in the UK. Judging by his glowing official obituary, his past in South Africa seemed virtually unknown. Or perhaps it was a function of the charity that mourners show to the dead.

When my piece was published, I received an email from a former ARM comrade of Leftwich's. I'll call him Mr X.

'The reason I'm emailing you is to correct a couple of important errors,' he wrote.

Leftwich was never beaten after being taken into custody, Mr X claimed. Not a finger was laid on him. He 'gave the names', including that of his girl-friend, almost immediately after being arrested with incriminating documents in his flat.

It would have cost Leftwich nothing to concede various points when testifying against his former comrades, Mr X added. 'He refused, despite cross-examination, to yield an inch to help.'

I was confused. These details seemed so at odds with the tone of Left-wich's essay in which he expressed such penitence. The essay was confessional; his soul laid bare. He said he had been trying to write it for over a decade. One of the close friends who Leftwich betrayed, activist Hugh Lewin, wrote of being deeply affected by the essay.

I received another email, containing an anecdote told to the writer by a former student who had been enrolled at York, where Leftwich taught.

'He said that there was a charismatic lecturer at York who was a former "freedom fighter" from South Africa, who had been betrayed by his com-rades and had managed to escape from the clutches of the police and get out of the country by the skin of his teeth,' the person wrote.

'I asked what his name was, and the student said "Dr Leftwich". I said that some minor details of this story might have been distorted in trans-mission, and I asked who had told him all this. He said: "Oh no, it's all true! I was told it by Dr Leftwich himself."'

How are we to make sense of this? Of Leftwich not only misrepresenting crucial details of his own act of sabotage, but potentially presenting him-self as the wronged hero in an alternative story of his own making?

Adrian Leftwich betrayed his comrades, his friends, his girlfriend. Oth-ers in his situation did not. That is beyond dispute.

'Slowly but surely I spilled the beans,' Leftwich wrote.

Trying to start a new life overseas, by his own account, he was racked by shame and guilt. In writing 'I Gave the Names', almost 40 years after the events he describes, he seemed to be desperately seeking a kind of absolution, however scant.

'I have come to believe not only that it is possible to go on and to keep going, but that we should and we must,' Leftwich concludes.

'There is simply no other way to be: to remember and take responsibility for the past in order to live in the present and contribute to the future; to learn from that past so as never to be like that again; to pass it on.'

But what if that confessional essay is, in a number of significant aspects, untrue? If Leftwich is *not* taking 'responsibility for the past', as he claims is his goal?

I don't know if my email correspondents were telling the truth. I didn't write a follow-up to my article, partly because the news cycle had moved on, and partly because I didn't want to cause Leftwich's mourning family further distress.

I suspect, though, that my email correspondents might have less motive to lie than Leftwich did.

I wanted to believe 'I Gave the Names' because it rang so true to me about what someone would do in a position of desperate fear for their lives. It didn't excuse Leftwich's capitulation, but I could understand it better. If you can't, you're a braver person than I.

'No one really knows how he or she will react when faced with those kinds of pressures,' Leftwich writes.

'I have often wondered why we do not know how we will react. Is it because we do not know ourselves sufficiently well?'

I know myself well enough to believe that I might crack in the face of losing my life or having the lives of those I love threatened. But what if that threat was never on the table for Leftwich? How are we then to understand his betrayal?

I don't know the answer to that, and I don't know if any reason could satisfy us.

27

Reality Bites

Let's take a trip back to October 2000 in South Africa, when the controversy over Aids denialism was reaching its peak and President Thabo Mbeki was accepting counsel from a panel touted as dissident 'scientists'.

The dissidents claimed not only that HIV did not cause Aids, but that antiretrovirals, in fact, were responsible for the inoculation of the constellation of diseases we term 'Aids'. And to attempt to prove the point, one of these 'scientists', the notorious Californian David Rasnick, challenged a prominent South African public health doctor, Costa Gazi, to a 'public experiment'.

It wasn't really an experiment at all. What he was proposing was effectively a medieval duel.

This is what he suggested: live on international television, Rasnick would be injected with 'purified HIV'. Simultaneously, Costa Gazi would begin a lifetime course of antiretroviral medication. Then we, the public, would watch and wait to see which one lived longer and which one developed Aids and died.

Sensibly, Gazi did not accept. But there is a part of me that is sorry he turned down Rasnick because it would have made a *riveting* reality show. Obviously a tad on the ghoulish side, watching Rasnick wither and die, but I'd save my tears for the people prevented access to ARVs in South Africa at least partly because of his so-called counsel.

'Pshhht,' you may say. 'That reality show would never get made. What kind of a world do you think we live in?'

Allow me to answer that with reference to a number of other reality TV shows produced over the last decade.

Exhibit A: *Who's Your Daddy*, a US reality show given the green light by Fox in 2004, in which a young woman adopted as a child had to guess who her real father was after interacting with eight strangers. If she got it right, she got $100 000.

If she picked the wrong guy – which is to say, if she was tricked by the producers into perceiving an emotional connection with a man she desperately hoped might be her father – he got $100 000. Everybody wins! This is also the plot of *Mamma Mia*.

Exhibit B: From the lovely folk at Fox, around the same time, a reality show called *Seriously, Dude, I'm Gay!* This show was advertised as featuring 'very straight men' – that means men who really, really love sex with females – trying to convince their loved ones and strangers that they were actually gay.

My girlfriend once did the opposite to her mother. One April Fool's Day, she rang her up to announce that she had decided she was straight. A risky little prank, with obvious backfire potential. Imagine if her mother had started sobbing with joy and relief? Thankfully, she lashed out in anger. 'Gay! Straight! Gay! Straight! Which is it?' she hissed, not unreasonably.

Anyway, on *Seriously Dude, I'm Gay!* the contestants would 'immerse themselves in the gay lifestyle'. What the producers had in mind here was basically 'shopping and going to gay bars', rather than 'experiencing systemic discrimination in most parts of the world'. At the end of the show, expert gays – that means men who really, really love sex with other men – would award the guy they thought was gay $50 000.

Activist gays got cross about the contestants telling everyone that pretending to be gay was their 'worst nightmare' and that they had been 'trapped in gay hell', so the show never made it to air after the pilot was produced. But it *almost* did!

Exhibit C: *Married at First Sight*, which debuted on American screens in 2014. This exciting new low for TV dating shows saw complete strangers meet for the first time and instantly get married, before exchanging a word to each other, after being paired together via 'scientific' matchmaking.

One of the contestants explained: 'My siblings were like, "Jamie, you're never going to get married if you don't do something like this, so go ahead."' Six months down the line, one couple was already divorced, while the other two were hanging on for a spin-off series.

And people say *gays* are destroying the sanctity of marriage.

Exhibit D: *Women's Logic*, a 2012 Georgian TV show that should really have been called *Chicks: How Thick are they Really?* Here teams of men were asked to guess what kinds of dumb answers beautiful women would give when asked general knowledge questions. The women always got it wrong, presumably because they were selected for being mentally sub-normal.

When faced with a picture of Salvador Dali and asked to identify him, two models decided that he was a 'hair stylist'. Cue raucous amusement and fist-bumps from the intellectually well-functioning men chosen to go up against them. There were protests that the show could harm job prospects for all Georgian women.

I haven't seen any of these shows, but to be honest, if I was given half the chance I'd watch the shit out of them. With a disapproving air, needless to say, but a disapproving air that might be hard to perceive while I shhhhh'd everyone in the vicinity and shovelled popcorn into my mouth.

I watched the entire season of a 2014 game show called *I Wanna Marry Harry*, which featured 12 young American women competing with each other to win the heart of a posh, red-haired English bloke *who was pretending to be Prince Harry*.

These women actually swallowed the idea that the fourth in line to the British throne had been given permission to participate in a reality TV show in which he would choose a potential princess from brash American commoners.

The dude posing as Prince Harry didn't even look like Prince Harry. But judging by the evidence of the show, you could possibly shove a ginger mop on top of a cardboard box and American girls would think they were hanging out with Prince Harry. When they were eliminated, they bawled: 'At least I got to meet Prince Harry.'

I'm also partial to the UK show *Dating in the Dark*, which takes three men and three women and allows them to meet, initially, only in complete darkness. The idea is that they will make decisions about who they'd be most romantically suited to based on quaint factors such as personality. And indeed they do. 'He sounds really lovely,' an absurdly beautiful girl will chatter away. 'She just seems really cool,' a beefy hunk will nod.

But the old adage that love is blind is exposed as a monstrous hoax the minute the lights go on and they can suddenly see each other. The 'really lovely' potential mate is a pot-bellied young man with terrible teeth. The 'really cool' future lover is a nerdy-looking woman with limp hair. And oh, how quickly they backtrack – the women as fast as the men. The memories of all that electric banter in the dark, that sense of a meaningful connection, immediately evaporate.

Of course, they can't really say, 'I've changed my mind because he/she is not hot enough.' They employ torturous euphemisms, transparent circumlocutions. 'I'm just looking for someone a bit more … confident in their own skin,' they'll manage.

I've yet to see a single episode where someone was selected for their sparkling personality, turned out to be less attractive than hoped and nonetheless stayed as their potential date's top choice. It's a bleak indictment of the dating economy. I think I'd rather go on the show where you get married immediately. At least the other person is contractually obliged to go through with it.

There's a show called *Freaky Eaters*, which is also on my must-watch list. One episode was about an American woman named Mysti who was addicted to tartar sauce.

'I haven't been on a date for five years,' she said despairingly. 'Tartar sauce has taken over my life.'

She ate tartar sauce on her cereal in the mornings. She ate it on red velvet cupcakes. She ate it on spaghetti. She kept emergency bottles of tartar sauce in her handbag and her car.

Mysti received a week of intense treatment for her tartar sauce addiction. 'She is powerless over this substance,' said a specialist. He told her: 'You've crossed that line between using tartar sauce to feel pleasure, to needing it to feel normal.'

'It's delicious,' Mysti said sadly.

The specialists poured 120 litres of tartar sauce into a kiddies' pool, because that was how much of it Mysti ate per week. Then they made her get into the pool. Promisingly, Mysti didn't start funnelling the stuff into her mouth. She said 'Eww'. It seemed like an unorthodox form of therapy to me, but by the end of the show she felt able to leave the house without a bottle.

I hope Mysti didn't relapse when the cameras stopped rolling.

The future reality show that I'm most invested in is the one that proposes to send four people to Mars in 2024. The Dutch Mars One project is funding its entire space mission by what it claims will be the most audacious reality show ever.

The application process began in April 2013, when Mars One announced that it was looking for four people to establish a colony on Mars. After the producers have weeded applicants down to six teams of four, the reality show will begin. The would-be astronauts will undergo training in a setting created to mimic Mars, watched by the world, and then the public will vote on who to send on the first mission to Mars.

This is all, by the way, *completely serious*. I've signed up for their mailing list so I'm kept abreast of their developments.

As of May 2014 the producers have a sifted-down pool of 705 potential Mars settlers. Of these applicants, 19 are from South Africa. It's interesting that so many people are eagerly competing for a shot at the mission because the humans who get sent to Mars are never coming back. It's a one-way trip. They won't have the technology to send anyone home to Earth. The Mars One website addresses the issue in an impressively blasé fashion.

'Because our astronauts are likely to spend the rest of their lives on Mars it follows that they will probably pass away there as well,' reads their FAQ on the matter. 'When that day comes there will be a memorial service and cremation ceremony.'

And imagine the ratings for the TV show when they die! After all, life in the Mars colony will be broadcast on an ongoing basis. People will be rushing home from the office to check what those crazy settlers are up to.

But, I discovered with great disappointment, there will be limits to the footage.

'Mars One would not allow 24/7 coverage ... the people of Mars wouldn't allow it,' the project's director Bas Lansdorp explained at its launch. 'If they don't like a particular camera, they'd put a piece of duct tape over it and there's nothing we can do about it. They are in charge.'

But, but ...What if one of the astronauts puts a piece of duct tape over the camera because she's about to kill the other three and eat their faces? That would be the best part and all we'd get is a black screen with some munching sounds. They need to think this through more carefully.

The Mars settlers may kill themselves before killing each other, though, because life on Mars is going to be totally shit. The average temperature varies between –87° and –15° centigrade. Martian years are 687 days long. Imagine how carefully you'd have to consider your New Year's resolutions. It would be the same thing every year: 'Do not kill self or others.'

They'd also be rarely able to leave their settlement because Mars has dust storms that rage for months at a time. Not that there's much to see when you do get out there. No water. No vegetation. The planet does have a mountain that is three times the height of Everest. That's something, though you'd be hard pressed to build a whole tourism campaign around it.

What potential settlers *would* be able to do, however, is communicate with people back home. Mars One claims that with the appropriate communication satellites, these guinea pigs will be able to use WhatsApp and Skype. On average there will be a seven-minute delay, but this will be no sacrifice for those used to Cell C.

The other thing the Mars One producers might want to give a teeny bit more consideration to, however, is the idea that the public is best placed to select astronauts to colonise Mars. We already have evidence of how crap the public is at making these important decisions because the best singer *never* wins Idols. And who would vote for the boring, stable candidates? We're the ones who have to watch them set up their bloody Space colony.

What we'd want is exactly what makes every other reality show compelling: dysfunctional relationships and boozy misbehaviour. We all know she couldn't colonise a bar stool, but I'd vote for someone like Snooki from *Jersey Shore* to go – a borderline alcoholic with poor impulse control and a tendency to overshare. Houston, we have a ratings winner.

28

A Lot of Hot Air

In many religions hell is seen as diabolically hot. Not all, though. There are others where hell is conceived of as icily cold or permanently wet. I'm tempted to say that I would always rather experience a hell where it is too hot than too cold or too wet, but obviously *it depends*. We are presumably talking about a situation where you can never cool down, warm up, or dry off. But neither can you ever die of over-exposure to these conditions, which complicates matters a bit.

When it's really hot there's an observable spike in crime rates, supposedly because agitation rises with adrenaline and testosterone levels. Winter depression and tiredness during cold, dark weather is well-established in Nordic countries.

Perpetual rain is also said to induce gloominess. There's a really haunting short story by sci-fi writer Ray Bradbury called 'All Summer in a Day'. It's set on the planet Venus, where – in Bradbury's version – the sun only appears for one hour every seven years. The rest of the time it rains. A group of school bullies lock a classmate, Margot, in the classroom closet one day. And then the sun appears. Overjoyed, they caper about, unaccustomed to the warmth and light. As the first raindrop hits, they scurry back inside. Only then do they remember Margot in the closet, doomed to wait another seven years to feel the sun's rays.

This tragic tale could also be a documentary about daily life in parts of England.

It seems that in a really hot hell everyone would be angry all the time, and in a really cold or rainy hell everyone would be permanently depressed. But we have to allow for the fact that regardless of climate everyone would be angry and depressed anyway because they're in hell.

It's sort of hard to imagine, but over millennia – we're talking about eternity, after all – wouldn't you get used to extreme weather conditions just a little bit? Even when they're not in hell, humans have adapted to life in places they have no evolutionary business being, such as blazing deserts and the unforgiving Arctic Circle.

I've often wondered whether hell would be standard for everyone or personally tailored towards the conditions you find most disagreeable. It makes sense that it should be the latter.

I saw a *New Yorker* cartoon once of demons ushering a man and his wife into hell – which turns out to be a palm-fringed length of idyllic coastline. 'I should have known,' the man says bitterly to his wife. 'I *hate* the beach.'

I understand the concept. Who's to say that my idea of hell is the same as yours?

If priests and theologians really wanted to scare me into unimpeachable behaviour on Earth, they'd paint a vision of hell that is predominantly windy.

As I write this, a South Easter is violently raging outside my flat in Cape Town. It will carry roofs off shacks. It will shatter the windows of apartments close to the mountain. Some days you can't walk in it. The wind folds you in half, makes you scurry doubled-over from one clutching-post to the next, pieces of grit stinging your eyes.

They call this wind the Cape Doctor because it was reputed to blow germs out to sea. In reality, it strews chip packets and newspapers all over the streets. The Cape Doctor is a ridiculously positive name for this diabolical gale. It should be named something more fitting, like 'Satan's Roar'.

The windiest place in South Africa is apparently not the so-called Windy City – Port Elizabeth – at all. It's Cape Point, where the South African Weather Service estimates only 2% of all the hours in a year are calm.

By my calculations, that means you only get seven wind-free days annually. An eternity in Cape Point, despite its magnificent views, would be close to my idea of hell.

Some people like wind, I know. They like the sense of exhausted exhilaration once they've finished battling it, and the sense of catharsis once the air stills again. To me, this is a bit like the man who was asked why he was banging his head against the wall, and replied: 'Because it feels so good when I stop.'

I heard about a Scout master who refused to take kids out when the wind blew. He said it did something to their mood that made them impossible to control. I can believe it. Wind makes me feel edgy and unsettled. It's my least favourite element, but also, I think, the most enigmatic. I like reading about the characters of different winds.

In central Europe they have a wind called the Föhn, which sounds a bit like what we call the berg wind in South Africa: dry and warm. At one stage, it was the most-studied wind in the world.

Hitler's photographer Heinrich Hoffmann, who wrote a book cheerily titled *Hitler Was My Friend*, recounted how Hitler was feeling in a disturbed mood one evening in September 1931, and Hoffmann tried to convince him it was because the Föhn was blowing.

As it turned out, it was because Hitler's niece had died, which shows how much Hoffmann knew.

Hitler used to ask Hoffmann to take pictures of him waving his hands around before he gave speeches, so he could see how the gestures would look to the crowd. You can find examples of the photos online. Hitler looks like a slightly comical mime: pointing, thrusting, holding both fists up to his face like a drunk man ready to box. I guess his poses must have been more effective in the flesh.

Hoffmann thought the Föhn might have been responsible for Hitler's weird mood, even though one imagines that the Fuhrer was quite often in a weird mood, because Föhn winds are believed to induce everything from migraines to psychosis. There's a word for the phenomenon in German: *Föhnkrankheit*. Wind-sickness.

In traditional Chinese medicine, too, wind is considered a major cause of illness.

In southern California they have a strong, dry wind called the Santa Ana, sometimes known as the 'devil wind'. Locals claim it makes people more anxious and aggressive. Canada has the Chinook, said to cause irritability and sleeplessness.

In *The English Patient*, Michael Ondaatjie writes of the mysterious winds of North Africa. The *aajej*, 'against which the fellahin defend themselves with knives'. The secret wind of the desert, 'whose name was erased by a king after his son died within it'. The *simoom*, a wind so enraging that an ancient nation declared war on it.

France and Switzerland have a dry, cold wind called '*la bise*'. Chris de Burgh writes about it in a song called 'Lonely Sky', a melancholic little ditty I like to sing when I've had a bit too much to drink.

When *la bise* blows in summer, they say: '*avec la bise, lave ta chemise*' – when the *bise* blows, wash your shirt.

The Loo is a North Indian wind, which Salman Rushdie described as a 'hot afternoon breath-that-chokes', carrying disease and madness. People eat special sherbets and drink *lassi* to protect themselves against the effects of the Loo.

I'm fond of winds with evocative names. The Williwaw, which wreaks havoc in sudden gusts on ships in the Strait of Magellan. The Coromuel, a strong warm wind in Mexico named after Samuel Cromwell, a British sailor whose name the locals struggled to pronounce.

Spain's Matacabras is as vicious as it sounds: 'the wind that kills goats'. I'll take the Zephyr instead, gentlest of all winds, named after the kindly Greek god who came in springtime and melted snow.

Car manufacturers like naming vehicles after winds, presumably for the connotations of speed rather than destruction. Ford brought out a Zephyr; the Volkswagen 'Passat' is the German word for a trade wind. There's a Maserati Mistral, after the cold north-westerly that blows in southern France.

If they named a car after the Cape Doctor, I think it would look something like an old Datsun, screaming recklessly around corners blasting house music, its inhabitants pitching beer cans out of the windows as they drove.

It seems wrong to me that the term 'the doldrums' referred originally to a period without wind, because its metaphorical meaning remains negative.

You can understand it when you consider that the term arose in the context of 18th-century shipping, when to be stuck without wind meant to be trapped in one spot. Today when we say we are 'down in the doldrums' we still mean that we're mired in a period of depression, lethargy, stagnation.

I might reclaim the phrase, as a wind-sick Capetonian, to refer to a state of blessed tranquility.

'We're in the doldrums today,' I'll say. 'How about a picnic?'

29

Different Strokes

You know, as a proud gay person, you *think* you practice an 'alternative sexuality', and then you find out about objectum sexuality.

Objectum sexuals fall in love with inanimate objects. And not in the way that, say, you might be fond of your car. A woman called Erika Eiffel, who self-identifies as an objectum sexual, founded a website to try to raise awareness of this sexual preference, and try to reduce stigma.

'We love objects on a very significant level and many of us in an intimate way,' she writes.

Objectum sexuals start developing feelings towards objects around puberty, in the same way that many of us wake up to the appeal of boys and girls at that time.

Sometimes the objects they fall in love with are very famous public monuments. Erika Eiffel was not born Erika Eiffel. She was born Erika LaBrie, but she changed her surname when she married. Perhaps you see where this is going.

Erika met her future spouse in Paris in 2004. Tall, grey and handsome.

'Everyone was all bundled up and I felt so warm inside,' she told Canada's *Globe and Mail* some years later. 'I thought, I don't feel cold, I feel so much warmth coming from the Eiffel Tower.'

Three years later, Erika married the Eiffel Tower in a ceremony attended by ten of her closest friends.

Being in a relationship with a very high-profile landmark carries its own challenges. Erika, who is American, would reportedly fly to Paris as often as possible to spend all day touching the Eiffel Tower.

You imagine that that's hard to do without attracting some interested glances. On the other hand, people who aren't objectum sexuals often behave in a similar manner around objects that have particular significance to them.

I once visited the holy shrine of Loreto, in Italy. There's a cathedral there which houses the reconstructed home where Mary was living when the angels came and told her she would give birth to Jesus. They transported the bricks of the house from Nazareth to Italy during the Crusades, fearing for its safety, and rebuilt it.

I liked the fact that there was some Jesus-era graffiti carved into the bricks. I can't read Aramaic, obviously, but I'd like to think it said something like 'Nobody talk to Judas OK'.

Beyond this, though, I must report that to atheist eyes, the whole spectacle was a little bit *weird*. That's because there were a lot of people with their eyes closed ecstatically rubbing themselves against the bricks. I'm pretty sure they might be the same people who wouldn't be inclined to look kindly upon Erika Eiffel.

But back to Erika. She notes on her website that one of the difficulties of loving a public monument is, obviously, that the necessary kind of access to it is tricky. She suggests that 'working for or around the object' is one way to get past that, though I'd imagine that HR might feel differently.

Otherwise, she proposes building or acquiring a scale model. It's a poor substitute to the actual hulking virility of the Eiffel Tower, needless to say, but she suggests that it's 'similar to people carrying photographs or articles such as jewellery to remind them of their distant lover'.

It's a bit easier to fall in love with something less ambitious. Perhaps even an object you can keep around the house. Erika's first love was an archery bow called Lance. Is it coincidental that Erika is a former world champion archer?

Many objectum sexuals are polyamorous. Erika is no exception, because the other big relationship in her life is with the Berlin Wall. In fact, the Wall was always the one that she really wanted. The Eiffel Tower was a sort of rebound thing. In a later interview with *SoSo Magazine*, Erika explained: 'I thought it was really important for me to pull away from the Wall, tie the knot and settle down.'

But marriage to the Tower forced her to confront her true feelings for the Wall. 'I finally broke down and I had to admit that I loved the Berlin Wall,' she said.

Erika and other objectum sexuals are adamant that their relationships with objects are mutual. This is one of the hardest things to understand as an outsider.

'There are cases of love being one-sided as with any orientation, but in general we do feel love in return,' Erika has written on her website, and she has underlined the last bit for emphasis.

I've been trying to think about which objects in my life I have the most significant attachments to. My most passionate relationships are with the devices I depend on for communication – my cellphone and my laptop. But in both cases the dominant emotions are hatred and frustration.

I have a teddy bear called Bearsley who I feel very fondly towards, as he is a noble little bear who wears a cravat, but I've never been tempted to have sex with him.

Objectum sexuals don't seem to like discussing sex though many of them are physically intimate with their objects. 'People think that all OS people have no regard for decency, that we're all severely traumatised or that they have to worry about us humping their garden fence or something,' Erika told *SoSo Magazine*.

It is very hard to read about Erika Eiffel without feeling that one has inadvertently taken a lot of acid. But there is nothing remotely surreal or funny about the situation to Erika or other objectum sexuals.

When I consider objectum sexuals my overwhelming feeling is one of relief that I am not one. Can you imagine being a kid hitting puberty and while all your peers are salivating over pop stars and actors you are secretly pining after a bridge?

I understand why objectum sexuals are the subject of quite a lot of curiosity, though I'm perplexed about why they are so stigmatised. It's not like they're doing any harm. If Erika wants to spend her afternoons engaging in some light frottage against the strats of the Eiffel Tower, I see no reason why we shouldn't let her get on with it.

From this perspective, maybe objectum sexuality is one of the better alternative orientations to be stuck with.

I'd rather be an objectum sexual than someone who experiences an overwhelming desire to have sex with animals, for instance. *Those* guys are in serious trouble.

Bestiality is mostly illegal, due to the widespread belief that animals cannot consent to sex with a human. Zoophiles – or 'zoos', as they call themselves – disagree. They maintain that it's simplistic to believe that the only way sexual consent can be registered is through human language.

I read an interview with a zoo in *New York Magazine* recently that I don't think I'll ever be able to get out of my head. The zoo in question came across as intelligent, rational and well-educated. Horses were his thing. He said that at the time when his peers were stealing their fathers' copies of *Playboy*, he was furtively flipping through *The Big Book of the Horse*.

The zoo was married to a human woman. An exceptionally understanding human woman, apparently, because he was also in a relationship with a horse he called Sexy Knickers. On their anniversary each year he would feed her extra apples as a treat. He said he wished he could be more open about their relationship. 'I'd love to say, "This is my girl, and she's on my arm,"' he said.

The zoo and Sexy Knickers had sex at least once a week. He claimed it was entirely consensual and mutually pleasurable. He also said he could tell if she wasn't in the mood, and then he wouldn't pursue it.

The journalist who conducted the interview asked incredibly fascinating questions in an entirely neutral manner, which you have to admire. At the end he asked if the zoo sometimes wished the horse could talk, especially when it was acting distant.

No, the zoo replied. 'I like the way we can partner without speaking,' he said. 'If she could talk that would make her less of a horse.'

I forced my girlfriend to read the interview because I desperately needed someone to discuss it with. She's still ranting about it.

'Oh, so he doesn't want the horse to be able to speak?' she fumes. 'That's because he knows the horse would say GET THE FUCK AWAY FROM ME YOU FAT FREAK!'

I didn't feel the same way. I thought that – relatively speaking – the guy did a reasonably good job of at least *complicating* one of the greatest taboos in human society.

The difficulty is, of course, that there is no way of testing Sexy Knickers's alleged consent to sex. She hadn't kicked him in the head yet, which is something. He claimed she orgasmed but frankly I don't really want to get into that.

I didn't find all his justifications satisfactory. But one thing he did quite well was to expose the hypocrisy of the 'consent' argument when it comes to everything other than sex that regards animals.

We hardly ever ask animals for their consent for anything. We don't ask their consent to ride them, to tie them up, to race them, to milk them, to do lab experiments on them, or to kill them. I'm not totally convinced that having sex with an animal is leagues more traumatising for the beast than some of the other stuff we do to them without batting an eyelid.

Don't misunderstand me: *that doesn't make it right.* Just because we don't ask animals for their consent to kill them doesn't mean we should automatically be allowed to have sex with them without asking their consent. But I thought the zoo was correct to say that there is a certain hypocrisy at play here.

It is very, very difficult to have these conversations in an open way, outside of philosophy tutorials or debating competitions. Most people react with a deeply visceral disgust to bestiality because inter-species fornication is one of the original sins. (There's a good practical reason for this, by the way. It is not the possibility that you could become impregnated by a horse and give birth to a centaur. It is zoonosis: the transfer of disease from animals to humans.)

Bestiality is classed with paedophilia, as a pathology rather than an orientation. It's the same group that homosexuality was also lumped into not so long ago. Since sexual relations between two consenting same-sex adults is a moral world apart from raping animals and children, many people now fortunately accept that this was deeply nuts. In sensible parts of the world, homosexual relationships are no longer perceived as particularly 'alternative' at all. That's how it should be, I think. But not all gay people seem thrilled about that.

I recently travelled to Sweden on a reporting trip to Stockholm Pride. The Swedish government had invited a bunch of journalists from around the world to attend one of Europe's largest and best-organised gay pride weeks so we could go back home to our benighted countries and tell them how to do gay rights.

We were a motley little crew, drawn mainly from places to which you wouldn't ordinarily plan a summer holiday. Kosovo, for instance. It was shortly after an Air Malaysia plane had been downed by pro-Russian rebels over Ukraine, and unfortunately our group included one journalist from Ukraine – Vira – and one from Russia, Elena. Tensions between Vira and Elena ran high almost immediately, after Vira announced to the group contemptuously that she liked to call Russian president Vladimir Putin 'Putler'.

Sweden is one of the most right-on places in the world when it comes to gay rights. Schoolkids and street sweepers drop words like 'transphobia' and 'heteronormativity' into daily conversation like they're discussing the weather. It sounds churlish to say this, but they can be a *teeny* bit smug about it. After the fifth day of having it strongly implied that Sweden was the world's foremost paragon of sexual equality, I found myself quietly muttering: 'Yeah, but we backwards South Africans legalised gay marriage three years before you.'

Not everyone in Sweden is a lentil-eating leftie. They still experience some gay hate crimes. But in general terms, being gay in Sweden seems utterly unremarkable. They have prominent gay priests and a special gay police organisation. At Stockholm Pride, the Swedish prime minister marched proudly waving a rainbow flag. It's no big deal.

But what we were struck by, watching the Pride parade, was how mainstream the gay culture appeared to be. There were many, many gay couples marching with prams and children. A Pride Park had been set up for the week, with stalls and bars and fairground rides.

'It is so *boring*,' groaned Yildiz, a Turkish journalist in our group. Yildiz refused to be identified as either male or female, so was on the more radical end of the ideological spectrum. 'It is like some sort of...*religious festival*.'

Yildiz scorned Stockholm Pride as vanilla and corporate. I got the sense that Yildiz didn't *want* gay people brought into the centre. Yildiz found life on the margins more exciting. S/he was deeply invested in the idea of a fundamentally alternative sexuality. The idea of gay people being viewed as no less or more interesting or dangerous than heterosexuals seemed almost repulsive to Yildiz, who specialised in sexually provocative statements to the more straightlaced members of our reporting group.

Yildiz wanted gay people to have equal rights, and militantly so. But s/he didn't want equality as such. What Yildiz wanted was a world where gay people had equal rights, but weren't expected to conform to any conventional narratives of lifestyle or behaviour.

Yildiz's responses were, to me, the most interesting part of my trip. I liked Yildiz a lot, but I also recognised that the way we approached sexual orientation was entirely different. To Yildiz, being gay was a badge of honour, a rallying cry, and a profound and essential point of difference between him/her and most of the world.

I think being gay is one of the least interesting things about me – and undoubtedly that's because I have the money and privilege to move through the world largely unmolested about it. That seems like a pretty sweet position to me. Being co-opted into the mainstream, after all, is a future that objectum sexuals like Erika probably long for in vain.

30

Survival of the Witless

When I was a child, I walked around with a certain swagger in my step because whatever happened, I knew how to survive being swallowed by a python.

I knew this because I was a passionate reader of Willard Price's children's books about two young animal collectors, Hal and Roger, who travelled the world gathering exotic beasts for their father's zoo.

Those boys went everywhere: to Africa, to the South Seas, to volcanoes, to the Arctic. In retrospect I think their voyages were probably heavily tinged with racism – I'm thinking here particularly of 'Cannibal Adventure', set in New Guinea – but as dubious as Willard Price's anthropological insights might have been, I always trusted him completely when it came to animals.

Willard Price taught me what to do if a python has set its sights upon you. While your instincts might be urging you to run, that would be an amateurish mistake. Instead, you are required to lie flat as a pancake, your arms and legs pressed tightly to your sides, as if you're about to do a pin-jump into a swimming pool. You must then permit the python to begin to swallow you feet-first.

As the python sucks your legs into its body, you remain immobile. It is unsettling to watch a python ingest your lower half but you stay cool and relaxed because you know what's coming next. When the python is busily consuming your knees, you take your hunting knife, reach slowly downwards, and then *rip it in two* like you're opening an envelope.

'Sayonara, python,' you say after that, stepping out of its entrails and dusting off your safari suit.

I didn't have a hunting knife because I was ten years old and my father was a chartered accountant. But this struck me as a minor detail. The main thing was that I *knew what to do*, and I derived an enormous amount of quiet confidence from this fact.

Years later, to my horror, I found out that Price's advice was essentially a steaming pile of bullshit. For one thing, pythons apparently throttle you to unconsciousness before they try to eat you. For another, they normally start swallowing their prey head-first, rather than feet-first.

As such, lying stiff as a board smiling in anticipation of your sneaky envelope-slitting manoeuvre would seem rather foolish. Thank goodness I never had the chance to try it.

Much of my childhood reading prepared me for a world of terrifying danger, but not *useful* danger. I never read anything about what to do to repel a potential rapist, or how you know if someone's trying to clone your bank card at an ATM.

Instead, I was led to believe that quicksand, for instance, would pose a devastating threat to my adult life. If I knew one thing, it was that you could never be certain that a solid-looking surface would actually have the stability its appearance promised. It was almost always a trick.

There you'd be, wandering through the jungle, or across the beach, or down a suburban pavement, for that matter. One casual step and you were toast: sucked into a killer swamp that would tear you down to a suffocating death within minutes. The last thing your friends would see was one hand frantically flapping about the surface before it, too, was lost from sight.

People died like flies from quicksand in the books I read as a child. It was an epidemic.

I started thinking about this recently because I realised that I had never, in 32 years of life, ever read a news report of someone losing their life to quicksand. There was clearly a stunning dislocation between its prevalence in my childhood fiction and its real-life occurrences.

I'm obviously not the only person labouring under a misapprehension about the scale of quicksand incidents because one of the questions posed to Yahoo Answers is: 'How many people are killed by quicksand per year?' (The question underneath it is: 'Why are there no hot homeless people?', which gives you some idea of the average questioner.)

It appears that the answer is: None.

Apparently you *can* sink into sand or soil mixed with water but then your natural buoyancy will kick in. There is no way you could get entirely sucked into quicksand and die in that way, though you could die if you got stuck up to your waist and couldn't think of a way to get out of it and then a huge wave came along and drowned you.

But the scenario where you get sucked downwards like the last gush of water down a plughole? A lie. Just another gigantic falsehood.

I wondered if I was imagining how large quicksand seemed to loom over my childhood. I wasn't.

A writer at *Slate* carried out a survey of movies with some kind of quicksand sub-plot, and confirmed that its use was once massive. The peak of quicksand's hold on the cultural imagination appears to have been between the 1950s and the 1970s, where at one point nearly 3% of all films produced featured a quicksand scene.

In the 80s, when I was born, quicksand was already on its way out, but most of the books I was reading as a child were published in the preceding decades, which explains their quicksand-heaviness.

These days quicksand is frightfully passé. When *Slate* asked 10-year-olds in New York if they were scared of quicksand, one replied: 'It was before we were born. Maybe it will come back one day.'

So why did quicksand fall out of favour for novelists and film-makers? One theory is that they just overused it. The temptation is obvious. It's such an easy way to kill off a character. No explanation necessary, no complex set-up required. 'Quicksand!' someone screams, and you know they're done for, even if they're entering a boardroom.

Another is that Google oversaw its demise: the minute people could easily research the fact that quicksand was about as effective a killer as a Jacuzzi, they stopped buying it. 'Waaaait a minute,' these newly minted know-it-alls would say, as a character plunged to his swampy death. 'Objects can only sink to the level at which their weight is equal to the weight of the displaced sand and water!'

As with so many other subjects, the internet took our innocence, though also our fear.

Thanks to some online research I now know how to escape quicksand. All you have to do is lie back and float and gently paddle yourself to safety. It sounds almost embarrassingly easy, but I also cannot be certain that I'd be able to keep a sufficiently level head to do my backstroke to freedom if I was actually in that situation. I'd probably be thrashing around screaming 'Quicksand!' until I died of sheer exhaustion.

This gulf between rationally knowing what to do, and remembering to do it is what scares me most in these contexts. I used to watch a TV series called *Worst-Case Scenarios*, where every episode featured a perilous situation and taught you how to escape it.

The scenarios were always hugely dramatic, such as how to stop a runaway train or how to survive a volcanic eruption. I found the viewing process exceptionally stressful because I kept thinking that I should be taking notes, but was too lazy to do so.

Focus! I would berate myself. *The train is careening out of control, Davis! Apply the handbrake by pumping a lever in the vestibule between carriages!*

Of course, the chances that the task of stopping the runaway train would fall entirely to me seems rather remote. It's unlikely the other passengers would look around, see me reading my Kindle, and shout as one: *'That's* the gal for this job!'

Then again, you always think these things won't happen to you until they do.

'I'll never meet a python,' you say blithely. But I saw a horrifying documentary once called *United Snakes of America*, about a violinist who lived alone in an apartment on the Upper West Side of New York around the year 2000. It was a small studio apartment, crammed with sheet music and other possessions.

One day, rummaging through a cabinet, the violinist came across something that she initially thought was an enormous sheet of bubble wrap. But when she inspected it more closely, she realised it was a shed snake skin. She called in experts from a nearby zoo who confirmed that it came from a boa constrictor and had been shed within the past two weeks.

The experts turned that flat upside down but could find no trace of the snake. They advised the violinist to shake flour on to her small floor surface overnight. She obliged, and in the morning, clear as day, imprinted on the floor, there was the outline of a giant snake that had slid across the studio floor.

She was advised to keep a live rat in a cage in her apartment in the hope that the boa constrictor would wrap itself around the cage to get at the rat and in this manner reveal itself. *That was their best plan.* The experts' response was, in summary: 'Yup, your roommate is a boa constrictor, but we can't find the tricksy little bugger! Anyhoo, good luck and sweet dreams.'

A *New York Times* article from June 2000 confirms the story. The woman put up signs around her apartment block asking if anyone had lost a boa constrictor, but the superintendent made her take the signs down because they were 'making the other tenants too nervous'.

The article ended on a cliffhanger: would she brave New York's completely unaffordable housing market and leave, or would she stay? Would she have to tell the next tenants about the property's dirty little secret?

'As you can see, it's a compact little space, close to all local amenities, ample storage …There's a boa constrictor hiding somewhere, but *just look* at this magnificent parquet flooring!'

I haven't been able to find any information about what happened next though I did track down an obituary of the woman in question, Linda Fennimore. She died in 2013 – but of cancer rather than anything snake-related.

When I read her obituary I was glad that I'd had cause to research her, however, because she sounded like an amazing woman. I often find the obituaries of regular people much more interesting than those of celebrities because they sometimes include extraordinary details.

In the early 70s, Fennimore had survived a traffic accident that saw her hurled straight through a car's windscreen. She suffered a broken neck. Everyone told her she would never walk again, after an incompetent nurse moved her from her position in a hospital bed while attempting to change her sheets. Fennimore beat the odds. She not only walked again, but went on to a career as a celebrated jazz violinist. She was reportedly recorded in journals as a medical miracle.

She beat paralysis and she escaped a killer snake, only to be taken by cancer. I don't mean to beat you over the head with this, but … life, hey? Shoowee.

Now that I'm galloping towards middle age, what I long for is a textbook that tells you *not* how to survive pythons and quicksand, but how to negotiate the more mundane challenges of life.

How to graciously turn down an invitation without having to tell a monstrous lie, for instance. The perfect thing to say when someone presents you with their weird-looking baby. What to do when you've forgotten someone's name, and then you have to introduce them to a third party.

This is the shit I could really use some help with.

Books telling you what to do in these situations do exist, of course. They're called etiquette guides, but the problem is that traditionally they've been focused on helping you present yourself as a member of the upper class.

I couldn't care less if people think I'm a direct descendant of the tramp who goes through the bins outside my house. I just want a book, a TV show, or an app, that tells you how to negotiate sticky social scenarios without hurting anyone's feelings.

If only Willard Price had spent more time on that, and less time lying to me about pythons.

31

Desperately Seeking Mandela

I received the news that Nelson Mandela had died while I was in a nightclub.

And not just any nightclub, either. It was the kind of grim establishment that causes you to wake up the next day, peer blearily at the stamp on your wrist, and be seized by a compulsion to plunge your entire arm into hydrochloric acid to obliterate the stain.

uTata didn't struggle for that.

In retrospect, I'd do it differently. I'd be in a place of solitude and introspection when I got the news, cradled by the austere majesty of nature. Silence, and a wide sky of stars. I'd light a candle, or something, and stare out over this beautiful but tortured land, and muse on the weight of history and the fragility of human life.

Instead, I'm afraid I turned to my friend Roy and said: 'Shots. For Madiba.'

Then I hailed a taxi to take me home. My driver was an old white man. I felt sure that we were about to experience a moment of bonding that I'd carry with me in my heart for the rest of my days. It would probably end with us gently crooning the national anthem together, lost in our own thoughts.

'Nelson Mandela is … *dead*,' I slurred, turning the words over in my mouth to try to make sense of them.

He looked at me in his rear-view mirror. 'Mandela was a terrorist,' he said definitively.

I wish it had all happened differently. These moments always seem freighted with a kind of urgency and significance that your real-world circumstances almost never live up to.

But sometimes, just rarely, they do. There was a video that went viral in the immediate aftermath of Mandela's death, which showed two foreign tourists who were told of the news while they were queuing for the Robben Island ferry.

'Did you come especially for this day?' a journalist asks them, off-camera.

They look confused.

'For … uh … this tour?' one asks.

'Because of the passing away of Mandela,' the journalist says.

'Yes,' the other replies confidently, but you can tell she didn't grasp the real meaning of those words. 'We came just to see what he went through.'

They talk a little more, about tickets for the ferry, and the meaning of Mandela to them. But the tourists are still discussing him in the present tense.

'How does it make you feel that you're here on *this* day?' the journalist persists.

'Well, it's a magnificent day!' one replies, beaming. 'It's sunny, and it's nice!'

It's clear that they're beginning to get a bit surprised by the length of the interview. *Is this what passes for news in South Africa?*

The journalist gives it one last push.

'Maybe a bit more specifically, how does it feel to be here just a few hours after his death?'

There's a pause.

'Wait, wait, wait,' one says, still smiling, but more tentatively. She cups her hand to her ear. 'We missed what you were saying before. Did you just … say …'

'That Mandela died,' confirms the journalist briskly. *This is why people hate journalists.*

'Huh?' says one, literally. Her mouth falls open.

'Haven't you heard?' says the journalist. 'You didn't know?' The camera is still rolling. *This is why journalists shouldn't be allowed out in public.* She gives a small laugh of awkwardness. 'He died last night.'

The tourists turn away, instantly overcome. The journalist continues to press them on how they feel. They're crying now.

It's easy to see why the video became a brief internet sensation, despite its voyeuristic intrusion on a moment of grief. Their response is so natural, so unfeigned and so genuinely heartsore. They're not even South African.

But I'm sure there must be other people who watched it and thought: Man, that's the way to find out. Ideally not while having a camera shoved in your face, of course. But to be actually queuing to visit the place where Mandela spent 18 of his 27 prison years confined to a tiny cell? To be already hyped up on the poignancy of what you're about to see and *then* hear that this behemoth of freedom is dead?

That's a moment. Those tourists will be telling that story for the rest of their lives. I generally have to lie about the nightclub thing.

I feel like the question of where you were when you heard of the death of a global icon used to carry a lot more significance. My mother can still tell you about the moment she realised JFK had been assassinated. It's not a *classic* anecdote. It's not like she was in the White House. She was sitting alone reading at a pavement café in Paris, but that still sounds sort of glamorous and 60s-ish.

Nowadays, 90% of the time I'd be forced to answer the question of 'Where were you when you heard ...' with: 'On Twitter.'

I've never had a good historical moment. I was watching TV at home when I found out about Princess Diana dying. I was sitting in a kombi at a petrol station in Hout Bay with my friend Tarry, eating chips, when I heard about 9-11. I was drinking beer with my brother at a dive bar in North London when we learnt that Michael Jackson was no more, though I'm not entirely sure where would constitute a meaningful environment for that news. A theme park? A chimp sanctuary?

My friends Faith and Bianca were at the UK's most famous music festival, Glastonbury, when news broke about Michael Jackson. A woman they'd been talking to turned to Bianca and said, earnestly: 'You are my Diana moment.'

That's a bit weird, obviously, but there's something about these times that really makes you want to commune with total strangers. Your own friends and family just don't cut it. You want the desperate alienation of modern life to fall away, for a second, and be replaced with some form of mass catharsis.

North Koreans are the best at this, or the worst, depending on your perspective. Remember the scenes of terrible public grief when leader Kim Jong-il died in 2011? People standing in neat rows, just bawling. Some beat their fists against the pavement. Of course, there's some suggestion that their lives were at stake, but I bet they'd get home and feel sort of drained and peaceful.

I went to Cuba a few years go. I felt guilty because the whole time I was there I was secretly hoping that Fidel Castro would die. I kept thinking what a wicked anecdote it would make.

'Politics? Don't talk to *me* about politics. I was in Havana when Castro kicked it, you know.' Then I'd lean back in my chair and light a cigarette with a far-away, world-weary expression, as if I'd seen things I couldn't possibly discuss in polite company.

Every time I saw the slightest sign of an animated group of people talking together, I felt sure the moment had come. My guidebook told me that Cubans don't like to use Castro's name in conversation. Instead, they make the sign of a beard, or tap two fingers on their shoulders, to represent his military epaulettes. I scrutinised their every gesture hungrily, but I never saw anyone do that.

I burnt to discuss Castro with real-life Cubans. 'Hola, señor,' I wanted to say, casually approaching someone with a mojito. 'So how's it going with …' and then I'd make the sign.

But we were hamstrung by our lack of Spanish, and I was afraid of being thrown into a gulag by an undercover policeman. Or, worse still, tapping my shoulder with two fingers while making meaningful eye contact and having people think I was wiping away dandruff.

In our taxi on the way to the airport, though, we had a loquacious, English-speaking driver. We passed by an official-looking building. He gestured towards it.

'That is where Fidel lives now,' he said, just tossing the name out there without so much as bothering to make the sign of the beard. 'They make hospital for him in there.'

'Ooooh,' we breathed, noses pressed to the window.

'Sometimes he come out,' he continued.

'He crazy, sometimes he come out and walk around naked waving his arms wah-wah-wah.'

'Really?' we squealed, eyes wide as saucers, willing Fidel to do exactly that as we cruised by. *Imagine the Facebook photos!*

'No,' he said, without any sign of amusement.

We shrunk back into our seats, ashamed.

Castro didn't die during my trip. As if I'd get that lucky.

The days following Mandela's death were busy ones for journalists. I'm not sure why, because it wasn't like there was much actual news. I suppose we were all just desperate to capture that moment: the one anecdote, the one quote, the one photograph that would perfectly encapsulate the enormity of the nation's loss. As if anything could ever come close.

On the morning after he died, I went to a press conference at a smart Cape Town hotel given by Mandela's frenemy FW de Klerk.

I found myself alone in a lift with a woman who worked at the hotel. Her name badge was upside down.

'Your name badge is upside down,' I said. I'm not usually the kind of person who points out this sort of thing to total strangers. It was just that her upside-down name badge struck me as so poignantly emblematic of the sort of day it was.

She looked at me, and looked down at her name badge. I prayed she would say something like: 'Doesn't the whole world feel topsy-turvy today?'

She silently adjusted it.

Later that day I stood on the wind-blasted Grand Parade with friends, hoping to cry. I felt in desperate need of it. I craved that moment of collective release. But the prayers went on too long. The speeches from politicians seemed insipid and uninspiring. There weren't as many people there as I'd hoped, and nobody seemed to be publically weeping. There were no Pyongyang-like scenes of devastation; just a bunch of Capetonians standing around nodding polite 'hellos' to people they hadn't seen in a while.

I tried to focus on the specifics of Mandela's extraordinary life. The years when authorities tried to efface him altogether from the South African consciousness: his words forbidden to be quoted, his image forbidden to be shown.

Asimbonanga, as the song goes. We have not seen him.

I still couldn't cry.

I began to suspect that there was something wrong with me if I couldn't just sit quietly and contemplate Mandela's magnificent sacrifice and be moved to tears. Wasn't that evidence of some fundamental *lack*? Did I even have a soul? *Why couldn't I be more like those noble Robben Island tourists?*

Where I eventually found that electric sense of connection to the moment was in the free musical memorial to Mandela at the Cape Town Stadium. I still find it hard to describe without sounding like I'm pitching the concept for a cheesy mid-90s beer ad.

'Okay, so we'll have interracial lovers kissing, and Xhosa dudes singing in Afrikaans, and a white oke singing in Zulu, and South African flags flying as far as the eye can see and just everyone hugging and crying and stuff!' On paper, it sounds excruciating.

But I will remember it until I develop Alzheimer's.

It felt like the most profound and beautiful coming-together of a deeply fractured city.

At the end of the evening, as Ladysmith Black Mambazo's harmonies soared, the crowd took off the glow sticks adorning their heads and wrists and bound them together in an incandescent rope stretching nearly the length of the stadium. For that moment, the South Africa that Mandela wanted seemed real.

Nowadays it seems increasingly unfashionable to discuss Mandela without being seen to problematise his legacy. To disdain the manner in which he was packaged as a cuddly teddy bear to soothe white fears; to condemn his over-conciliatory attitude during the negotiations to dismantle apartheid. Much of this is undoubtedly valid, though the backlash has happened with bewildering speed.

A few months after Mandela's death I visited Qunu, his birthplace. I wasn't there on a pilgrimage. I was there to interview former miners who had developed lung disease and struggled to obtain any financial compensation.

I don't know what I was expecting Qunu to be like. Actually, that's not true. I know exactly what I was expecting it to be like.

'There is a lovely road that runs from Ixopo into the hills,' Alan Paton's

1948 novel *Cry, the Beloved Country* opens. 'These hills are grass-covered and rolling, and they are lovely beyond any singing of it.'

In my mind I think I had managed to conflate Ixopo with Qunu, despite the fact that the two places aren't even in the same province. There were grass-covered hills, and they were quite lovely. But the day was bleak and overcast, and what the hills were alive with was less the sound of music than the evidence of desolate poverty.

In a tiny house, I interviewed a man hobbled by disease contracted on the mines. He thought he would be able to work as a miner for a few years and then buy a tractor. Come back to Qunu, get some cows, be a farmer. Provide for his wife and kids. It's what Mandela would have wanted.

Now he is too ill to work. Even if he could, his chances of finding a job in this area are minuscule. As he spoke, his five children jumped up and down on a single bed they all share at night. From his house, you could see the home where Mandela spent much of his retirement. It was still closed for mourning.

I drove away feeling sad and tired, and about a million miles distant from that magical night at Cape Town Stadium where everything seemed tantalisingly possible.

On that grey afternoon, it was not *Asimbonanga* that stuck in my head. It was *Senzeni na*: What have we done?

32

Like/Dislike/Not Sure

Things I like: Music

Music is very useful. You can use it to drown out the sound of construction on the building opposite. If you play it loudly enough it hushes the little voices in your head that tell you you'll never amount to anything. It also fills the silence when you are on a long car journey with someone you don't really know. It is interesting that we speak of silence as needing to be 'filled', as if we lived in some kind of giant, empty jar. Which, in a way, we do, don't we? So we must fill the silence-jar with music-jam, and soldier on.

Things I dislike: When people tell you they are 'trying for a baby'

There should be a law against this. When someone tells you that they and their partner are 'trying for a baby' it forces you to immediately picture them banging. And it is never, say, George Clooney and Amal Alamuddin who confide in you in this way, since you would happily picture them copulating unprompted. The type of person who tells you this is normally a weird colleague, or someone you hated at school and just bumped into at Vida.

Things I like: Being a twin

In my experience twins are usually fascinated by the state of being a twin, because in childhood everyone tells you it's the most interesting thing about you. The most obvious advantage of being a twin is that you always have someone to talk to on your first day at a new school. It is also unlikely that you will ever forget your twin's birthday, and you never have to buy them a birthday present because it's your birthday too, goddammit. The only thing not to like about being a twin is when you communicate only with each other and turn to a life of crime and end up in a mental hospital, like Welsh identical twins June and Jennifer Gibbons. But even then people still want to write books about you, because you are extra creepy.

Things I dislike: When novelists tell you about characters' nightly dreams

When I am reading a book and the author insists on describing his or her character's dreams, I find it even more boring and irritating than when people tell you about their dreams in real life. It is, in fact, much more boring and irritating, because the author is just making it up, probably to fill a few pages. I deeply empathise with this urge, and if I could get away with it I would pad the rest of this book with a rambling imaginary account of a dream I never had, but my editors are too scary. The only occasion on which it is tolerable to hear about someone's dream is when you play a prominent role in it, preferably heroic. The worst parts in *Game of Thrones* are also when that spooky kid who has to be carried everywhere has dreams.

Things I like: Twitter

Twitter is much better than Facebook because it is not just about food and pictures of hen parties and inspirational quotes. You can tweet at famous people you admire and sometimes they tweet back, which makes you think that maybe being a famous person is less interesting than it seems. Often somebody on Twitter will say something racist or sexist or homophobic and then you all get to gang up on them and bully them until they repent. We are all only one ill-advised tweet away from a public lynching, which adds a thrilling frisson of danger to the whole thing.

Things I dislike: Video games

I don't dislike video games because they are breeding a violent society or perpetuating demeaning stereotypes about women. I dislike them because they are *so hard*. Seriously, have you tried playing a contemporary video game? They ain't like Super Mario no more. I always thought video games were created to provide teenage boys with a compulsive, brainless activity to engage in between bouts of compulsive, brainless masturbation. Then I tried to play Grand Theft Auto on the easiest level, and threw down the controller in tears of frustration. As far as I'm concerned, you need the manual dexterity of a Chinese seamstress paired with the steely mind of a NASA engineer. If you have a teenage son who spends hours on video games you should be rejoicing because it probably means he is a genius.

Things I like: Reading about other people's terrible experiences

I know this is morbid but I can't help it. One of my favourite non-fiction genres is the first-person accounts of young women who were abducted and kept as sex slaves. I also have almost an entire shelf dedicated to badly written books about people convicted of drug-smuggling and incarcerated in hellish Thai prisons. Schadenfreude literature has a valuable purpose because it makes you realise that your own shitty life is really quite peachy. It also teaches you never to talk to anyone sitting next to you on an airplane, in case they shove a small package of heroin into your handbag just before you land in Bangkok.

Things I dislike: The musical *War Horse*

Everyone loves *War Horse*. Saying you dislike it is akin to admitting you enjoy stubbing out your cigarettes on a puppy's soft head. Here I am, loud and proud: *War Horse* is *the fucking worst*. It's like being hit on the skull with a hammer made out of crystallised sugar for four hours with fiddle music droning in your ear while someone whines about their lost horse. 'But the puppets ... The puppets!' people cry. Yes, the puppets are impressive. They sure do look like real horses! It's not enough to support the maudlin sentimentality of a story that feels like something an old drunk would bore you to tears with at closing time in a rural pub. By the end of it I was rooting for the Germans.

Things I like: Dinosaurs

If *War Horse* was about dinosaurs instead, I would watch the hell out of it. Dinosaurs were the greatest of all animals because they took no shit from nobody and if you had tried to press them into service during wartime they would have sniggered while they ate you. I once met someone who found the world's most perfectly formed juvenile T-Rex skeleton and I was so jealous I almost cried, as well as somewhat sexually aroused. It is absurdly disappointing that dinosaurs' relatives are birds, because dinosaurs were so awesome and birds are so lame. For an analogy within *Homo sapiens*, see: Nelson Mandela and his grandchildren.

Things I dislike: Weather forecasts

Weather forecasts are ridiculously unhelpful. The gap between tomorrow's minimum and maximum temperature is always about 20 degrees. So it *might* be 10 degrees ... but it might also be 30 degrees. Thanks, guys! I guess I'll dress for work in a fur coat with a bikini underneath. When meteorologists get it wrong, there are also no negative consequences for them. In what other industry, beyond astrology and journalism, can you consistently provide false information to the public and keep your job? Maybe because only sailors and wedding planners actually really need a weather forecast. Just look out of the window tomorrow, dummies!

Things I like: Napping

I maintain a fundamental distrust for people who don't nap, because seriously, what is wrong with them? Non-nappers are often supercilious about their ability to maintain a strange, android-like wakefulness throughout the day. I attribute it to pure envy, since they perpetually have to find stuff to do, which must be very wearying. Professional nappers like myself never have to seek out activity of any kind, and as such are never bored. There is no time of day at which I could not be comfortably asleep within five minutes. I once worked in an office where everyone else went out for lunch every day, granting me 55 minutes of heavenly slumber on the office couch. When the door re-opened, I would have to jerk myself upright while wiping the drool from the cushions, and adopt a facial expression of manic alertness like someone on a three-day amphetamine bender. It was worth it.

Things I dislike: People who are snobby about coffee

It's coffee, okay? It's a hot drink made from a shrub, not the distilled tears of the Virgin Mary. I enjoy an invigorating cup of coffee as much as the next person. In fact, I own an expensive piece of specialist coffee-making equipment, but I secretly also find Koffiehuis quite scrumptious. 'Oh, you only have *instant*?' some people say, and wrinkle up their nose as if you've just offered them a pipette of your own urine. Being very particular about coffee generally goes together with a number of other quite annoying traits, like only drinking craft beer. I fail to see why things are considered intrinsically superior simply by virtue of not being produced in bulk. Maybe they're not produced in bulk because they're not delicious enough to warrant the demand? Ever think of *that*, Mr Snobby-Snob McCraftBeer?

Things I like: Protests

I think enjoying non-violent protest marches goes with the territory of being South African. It's one of our favourite national pastimes. Less so for white South Africans, though even they will take to the streets with a placard under the right circumstances, E-tolls, say, or a hike in the DSTV subscription fee. Cape Town protest marches usually traverse exactly the same route, from Keizersgracht to Parliament, which is a perfect distance because it's not long enough for things to get boring. I'll cheerfully protest against almost anything. In 2005 my friend Rebecca and I stayed in a protest camp outside Gleneagles to protest against the G8. Organisers taught us that if police horses started stampeding at us, we should stay seated but sway in an undulating motion to put them off their game. At that point I thought that perhaps I was in a bit too deep.

Things I dislike: Anti-rhino poaching fever

Don't get me wrong: I have nothing personally against rhinos. I wish them well as a species, and I think it's horrible that they die agonising deaths so that okes in Beijing can muster a boner. But I feel there is something downright disturbing about the hysteria with which rhino poaching is greeted, particularly by those South Africans who maintain a conspicuous silence on the country's other social ills. I think it is alarming that there are so often reports of poachers being killed by rangers and police, as if we have all just accepted that rhino poaching should be the only crime in South Africa punishable by the death penalty. I will also never accept it as equitable that rhino poachers sometimes receive harsher prison terms than murderers. Perhaps this makes me a human-supremacist, but I already knew that because I got really weirded out when the chimps in *Dawn of the Planet of the Apes* rode horses. It just didn't feel right.

Things I haven't made my mind up about: Children

Let's get real for a second. As an urban-dwelling individual, there is no good reason to have a child. You do not need an extra pair of hands at harvest time. You may be banking on being financially protected in your old age, but it's a risky investment given the huge economic outlay early on. There is no noble justification for breeding, unless you are depended on to re-populate the earth after a nuclear apocalypse. Having a child is probably the most damaging environmental act you can perform as an individual, other than running an oil tanker aground.

As far as I can see people want children because they want children, because they think the secret recipe of merged DNA between them and their partner will create a superhuman, because they want to correct the imperfections of their own childhoods, and because they secretly think they'll be better at child-rearing than anyone else.

Without meaning to sound like Scrooge McDuck, children can ruin your life. 'Children are certain sorrow and uncertain joy,' my father likes to say. He claims it's a Swedish proverb, which my Swedish mother denies, so maybe he just made it up, which is pretty telling in itself.

Having a child also makes you more fearful. It makes you more worried about the future, and the job market, and interest rates, and whether Julius Malema will expropriate all your unit trusts without compensation. Having a child forces you to contemplate what the world will look like decades from now, because your child will have to live in it. I can't even focus beyond the release date for the next season of *Orange is the New Black*.

But children also almost certainly make life richer, under the right circumstances. Christmas is about a million times more tolerable when children of whom you are fond are around. I fully believe that having a child is the most intense experience of love you can ever imagine. I believe, too, that having children can sometimes make you a better person – softer, and less selfish – though I share the incredulity of comedian Janeane Garofalo that people need to have a baby in order to realise 'it's not all about me any more'.

Children turn your grumpy old parents into gushing love-machine grandparents, if the experience of my own family is anything to go by. Infractions for which you would have been beaten like a drum as a child suddenly become loveable quirks when your parents turn into grandparents.

Sometimes I wish I had a baby because they make amazing social buffers. It sucks that you can no longer go out and party like Amy Winehouse, but babies also provide a perfect opportunity to leave boring social events early and decline unwanted invitations. Toddlers ensure that there are no awkward silences, because they are constantly doing shit that has to be observed or rewarded or guarded against. While you are the shield between your child and the world, your child is also the shield between you and the world. Let me pause here to say that I imagine that people who actually have children are reading this with escalating rage, because if there is one thing that people with children hate, it's when childless people give opinions about child-rearing. I fully get how frustrating that must be, but it seems a bit insane that it is only socially acceptable to opine on the pros and cons of having children *after* you've had one and can't give it back.

On the plus side, children are often hilarious and say the darnedest things. The best child who ever lived is my nephew Ben, who is an adorable genius who will definitely grow up to be an astronaut rockstar and rule the world. He calls Mary Poppins 'Mary Popcorn', and he is so cute that I want to eat him in one sitting dipped in soy sauce with some wasabi on the side. I am deeply grateful to my sister and her husband for creating him, because he makes my life better. That's a heavy burden for a two-year-old to have to shoulder, but his shoulders are uncommonly well-formed.

Being around Ben makes me wonder if I should have a Ben of my own. Gays can do that these days, you know. One of the best things about being gay in a homophobic world used to be that nobody expected you to meet any traditional social milestones, because if you made it to 30 without being a promiscuous junkie everyone was surprised and delighted. Now lesbians get married in meringue gowns at Boschendal and gay dudes are proud fathers by the time they're 28. It's tough out there.

The major reason I see for having a child, other than providing you with comic material to write about, is that they give your life a sense of purpose and meaning that you otherwise have to work quite hard to supply off your own bat. Having a child leaves little time for self-indulgent lying around wondering what the point of it all is. I envy that because as I forage deeper into the forest of my thirties I spend roughly 40% of my time lying around wondering what the point of it all is, sometimes while sucking on the teat of a papsak.

To give the necessary Best White disclaimer, this kind of navel-gazing is a hallmark of financial and social privilege, though it doesn't feel like much of a privilege.

If you don't have a child, you have to look elsewhere for meaning: in work, in relationships, in idealism of some form, or in 'hobbies', whatever those are.

If you die in an untimely fashion, nobody will find it as sad as if you had children. 'Father-of-three killed in terror attack,' newspapers like to trumpet. They know it makes it more poignant.

As you get older, people will ask, 'So you never wanted kids?' with an air of slight judgement, and you'll have to find a diplomatic response that doesn't automatically seem to disdain their own choices.

It's all very difficult, and at the time of writing I don't have any satisfactory conclusions. Please buy my second book, however, to learn all the answers. It will either be called *Trying for a Baby: Childrearing in a Non-Traditional Family*, or *Filling the Silence-Jar with Music-Jam: One Woman's Defiant Manifesto on Keeping Her Womb Empty and Her Heart Full*. Either way, I'll definitely need the money.

Acknowledgements

What I discovered in the course of writing this book is that writing a book is literally the worst. Fine, perhaps not 'literally' the worst. It is not like being a paramedic in Gaza, or one of the people who has to empty the sanitary bins in women's toilets. But it's bad.

It was a shattering blow to realise this, because I always thought that writing a book sounded like an absolute joke compared to 'actual work'. Wake up late, drink some coffee in a leisurely fashion while staring out of the window, put on a tweed jacket and roll into your book-lined study, bang out a few pages of peerless erudition, and then get an early start on the cocktails.

I don't have a book-lined study. I wrote this in our tiny, airless spare room. I'm not saying you should cry for me, because a lot of people don't even have a spare room, but my friend Roy once walked in and said: 'Do you seriously work here?', gesturing at my monastic wall in horror. I know now, at least, that if I were ever in prison I would churn out something of equivalent quality.

I apologise to my friends for being able to talk about nothing other than this book for half a year. Friends: you always said either the right thing or nothing at all about it, and I am going to thank you in full in case I never get another chance to write a book (as seems entirely likely), and also in case I never win an Oscar and don't get a chance to do that long boring speech.

For anyone writing a book, I wish them the clarity, kindness and surgical insights of my Pan Macmillan team: Andrea, Tanya, Terry, Laura and Babs.

Lauren, you gave me the push I needed when I was ready to drown, as did Darrel.

Eusebius and Osiame: Thanks for being consistently challenging bouncing-off posts.

My colleagues at the *Daily Maverick* have shown me everything I know about how to make sense of the world. I tell everyone I meet how rare it is to have colleagues whose company I enjoy as I do yours: Ranj, Jack, Bokkie, Styli, Simon, Marelise, Marianne, Poplak, Ant, Bheki, Brooks, Sisonke, John, Thapelo, Sipho and Khadija. Branko, I'll always be grateful that you took a chance on me.

Thanks to the good folk at Cape Talk, particularly John and Stephan, for tolerating my weekly presence. Thanks, too, to Carlos, Sue and the lovely team at the Sunday Times.

My Rhodes friends, you're the ones I know I can always turn to in a jam, but also to have a jam: Kimala, Nev, Stace, Sharon, Lise, Stevie, Sim and Paula.

Adam, Alex, Konstantin, KC: Meet you at the KA? Thank you for conversations that have helped shaped my views about tons of stuff.

Dr Pietsch, who changed my mind about many things and challenged me in the best ways possible.

Jess, who I've been chucking ideas around with since we were awkward teenagers.

Minnykins (aka Cristina): I approached much of this book as if I were having a conversation with you, so I hope you read it while drinking Lambrini.

Bec Hodes, to whom I owe an incalculable debt.

Michael and Roy, you endured the entire labour of this book and contributed so much to its content, but beyond that perpetually keep me sane and riotously entertained.

Anna Hartford, for giving me the title, the cover concept and many of the ideas, as well as being consistently brilliant and hilarious – I'm more grateful for your friendship than I can say.

Josie: Without the late-night WhatsApps, Highwayman renditions and everything else you do to make my life better, I would be a terribly sad little rat.

Tarry: Over 15 years, the most hilarious, inspiring and supportive friendship anyone can ever imagine. Someone should make a movie out of it. It would mainly be a comedy with about three dramatic parts, but everyone would leave the cinema feeling good, especially if they brought a hip flask like when we went to see *Bridesmaids*.

Thanks and love for everything to my family: Roger, Marianne, Mark, Peter, Rachel, Keegan and Ben.

Finally, to Jeanine, who has suffered through book-related rages, tantrums and tears, and has been my rock from beginning to end: soothing my anxieties, making my shit ideas better, and telling me I am not the worst writer in the whole world. Every writer should have a Jeanine, except that they can't have you because you're mine.